TIME TO AWAKEN

CHANGING THE WORLD
WITH CONSCIOUS AWARENESS

ORA NADRICH

This book is dedicated to my late father,
Shimon Zelig Rubinstein, and his entire
family who died in the Holocaust, along with
6 million Jews, and other innocent souls.

May we never stand idly by again.

TIME TO AWAKEN

ORA NADRICH

Published by:

IFTT Press

California, USA

Cover & Interior Design: Dmitriy Khanzhin

Editor: Julia Nugent

Author Photo Credit: Payam Arzani

A CIP record for this book is available from the Library of Congress Cataloging-in-Publication Data

ISBN: 979-8-9871638-1-8

Printed in USA

AS YOUR VIBRATION RISES,
FORCES WILL COME TO WORK AGAINST YOU.
THEY ARE AFRAID OF YOUR POWER. YOUR
SPIRITUAL AWAKENING SCARES THE SLEEPERS.

— UNKNOWN

WE SHALL MEET IN THE PLACE
WHERE THERE IS NO DARKNESS.

— GEORGE ORWELL, *1984*

Table of Contents

Introduction

When one realizes one is asleep,
at that moment one is already half-awake.

- P.D. OUSPENSKY

This book is intended for those who do not know that they are asleep. But, if you are holding it in your hands and you too are an awakened one, after you finish, please pass it on to anyone you may think is in an unconscious slumber, and does not know that a Great Awakening is upon us. For those of us that do know, we have been aware of this awakening for a long time, and acknowledge that this is why we are here on this earth — to awaken fully for the evolution of our humanity, which is in peril.

1

We also know that there has been a tremendous escalation in the awakening process, and the last few years ignited this awakening even more. It also revealed that too many people are still unaware of it, and are choosing, instead, to remain in a state of slumber out of fear.

Fear is the number one reason people stay stuck in ignorance, which means it's a choice. Awakening is something every human being can realize, but only if they desire to. The number one question to ask yourself at this time is, "Do I wish to fully awaken?" If your answer is yes, know that you made the right choice by reading this book. And, if you are someone who is already committed to the path of spiritual awakening, I hope you smile as you read each word in knowing familiarity.

Those that are on the path of awakening can recognize each other immediately. In our eyes, we see that we have transcended the fear that swept over the entire world, like a hypnotic trance, and those that chose fear over freedom are not awake enough to know it. We wish for them to join us on this life-changing journey of awakening. This is an extraordinary time to be alive, unlike any other time before it. I invite you, dear reader, to awaken with all of the warriors who have bravely gone beyond fear, knowing deep in their soul, the greatest freedom we have ever known, awaits us.

CHAPTER 1

Welcome To Awaken

We are all equally capable of spiritual awakening.

- VICTOR SHAMAS

Whether you are here by choice, someone gave you this book, you were intrigued by the title, or don't really know why you are here at this moment in time, I welcome you with wide, open arms, and a loving heart. You are about to embark on the most important journey of your life, and that is to awaken. I don't mean awaken from a night's sleep. I'm talking about awakening from a slumber that keeps you in a state of unconsciousness.

You see, from the moment you were born, you were groomed to be asleep to the sacred truths of this life, and most things you were told to trust and believe, until now, have contributed to you being more asleep than awake. "How can that be?", you might be asking. The answer is simple, deliberate unconsciousness. This is the state of being uninformed or unaware, and for the most part, we go through life being uninformed, or unaware of many things — until one day, if we are fortunate, something wakes us up like a sudden slap upside the head, and we think, "How could I have not known or seen that?"

What if I were to tell you that you are being intentionally uninformed to remain unaware so that you don't wake up to think, "How could I have not known or seen that?" By "intentional" I mean that, by design, we are kept in the dark about so many important, valuable, useful, and ultimately necessary things so that we can remain ignorant and dependent on others, but in fact, our ignorance is going to destroy us. You might be shaking your head and thinking, "That's ridiculous!", or "Who would do that to us?", or "Is this one of those conspiracy books?"

If you thought any of those things, that's perfectly natural. It's normal for the mind to default to disbelief when our beliefs are being challenged. How can you go through your entire life believing something is true, and then one day, someone comes along and tells you that what you have been believing is a lie? That probably seems so extreme and feels as if the carpet has been pulled right out from under you, and that's exactly what this book is intended to do. To pull you right out of your cozy, cushy, comfy zone, and stick you right into the coldest wake up shower you've ever taken.

Think of this as a reality ice-plunge. I'm sorry, but you

didn't think you were going to remain oblivious or igno-rant for this long, did you? If you're just now waking up to the idea that you've been duped into believing that every-thing you've been told is absolutely true, especially by the most powerful, "reliable" sources we've grown dependent on for our entire lives (until now), then maybe you should consider your need to have big mommy and daddy in the form of government, health organizations, and the pharmaceutical industry, (who pretty much run the show about every decision we make from what we believe, think, vote on, put in our bodies, or march to the tune of), then yes, you have lived your life dependent on being gov-erned rather than having self-ownership. I'm not saying you can't think for yourself, but to be a really sharp critical thinker means you must question everything, especially authority, which we are not quick to doubt when those in power tell us what we need to do to stay alive. And that's exactly what happened to us during what was called a "pandemic". We were told what to do to stay alive, even if what we were told went against our intuition, or seemed illogical.

By the way, do you know where the term "conspir-acy theory" comes from? There's a belief that "the CIA invented the term in 1967 to disqualify those who ques-tioned the official version of John F. Kennedy's assassina-tion and doubted that his killer, Lee Harvey Oswald, had acted alone. That's when the CIA put the words 'conspiracy' and 'theory' together to use as a tool of political propaganda" (Butter 2020). Apparently, there were many people who questioned the story of Kennedy's assassination, just like there are many people questioning what is being told to us by our government and health officials about the Covid-19 virus, and the pandemic, so does that mean we shouldn't question authority for fear of being labeled a conspiracy theorist? That seems to have been the case if you questioned anything that you were told during the pandemic. God forbid you asked questions! Many people, like myself, wanted answers to questions that just weren't being answered in ways we felt comfortable with. Please tell me what's wrong with wanting to know what was in the Covid-19 experimental shot? Is wanting to know what you're putting in your body because you are being told that you have to, or else you won't be able to work, visit loved ones, travel, buy groceries, eat in a restaurant, go to a sports event or concert, attend school, or even get a liver transplant, not something you have a right to know?

Let me ask you this. If I were holding a dark cup of liquid that you couldn't see, and said to you, "Drink this!", don't you think you would ask me, "What's in it?", which is perfectly reasonable. But, what if I were to answer, "I'm not telling you, but drink it anyway!", I would think you would say, "no." Why should you drink something I refuse to tell you what it is? Those are very logical ques-

tions to ask, but if you were someone who questioned
the Covid-19 experimental shot, you were immediately
judged, called an "anti-vaxxer", and for many, became estranged or ostracized from friends or family members. Do
you have any idea how painful that was for those who just
felt it was their right to ask questions about the Covid-19
experimental shot? And, whether they wanted informed
consent before taking it, had underlying health issues that
made them fearful of taking it, had spiritual or religious
reasons, or just did not want to take it for whatever
personal reasons they had, and have a right to, they were
put through unimaginable things, and made to feel like
a second class citizen, or a horrible person because they
were told by the government, and health officials (people
we are supposed to believe want to protect us, and have
our best interests at heart), that those people who refused
the Covid-19 experimental shot were out to kill others,
especially grandma!

Please take a moment to ask yourself if you were one
of those people who believed everything that was told to
you during one of the most difficult times in our history.
We were all very vulnerable, and susceptible to believing
whatever we were told. Did you feel judged or ostracized by
others? Did you judge or ostracize anyone because they had
a different opinion than you? Did you not feel that you had
a right to your personal feelings, or that someone else did?

Perhaps you were someone who believed you were

"following the science." That was one of the most over-used reasons we heard from people who believed they should take the Covid-19 experimental shot without questioning it, whatsoever, and if you're someone who did "follow the science", I have some questions for you:

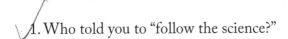

1. Who told you to "follow the science?"

2. Why did you believe them to "follow the science?"

3. Did you ever question the science, or just went along with it because you were told to, by an authority figure?

4. Did you "follow the science" for yourself, others, both, or for other reasons?

5. What is the science?

6. If you feel the Covid-19 experimental shot is the science, what is in the vaccine?

7. How would you explain "follow the science" to someone who doesn't know what it is, in the simplest way?

8. Do you feel you have a complete understanding of

what "follow the science" means?

9. If you were asked to "follow the science" again, would you do the exact same thing?

10. How do you feel about the science of the Covid-19 experimental shot today?

11. How has "following the science" changed, or improved your life?

Whether you followed the science, or never believed in it for one minute, it's very important for us to reflect on one of the most difficult, and challenging times we've ever gone through, and ask ourselves very important questions about what we're being told, and even mandated to do. Even though we're not in lockdown anymore (that could change), there are still many things happening that we must be very aware of, like the ongoing EUA (Emergency Use Authorization) that the FDA, and WHO (World Health Organization) are trying to extend with the Monkeypox virus (the newest virus that has mysteriously popped up, and I'm sure many more will too), which is a sexually transmitted disease on the rise in the LGBTQ community, and "being driven overwhelmingly by sex between men, major study finds"(Ryan and Lavietes 2022), but could very well be mandated for all of us to get, which like the Covid-19 experimental shot, has not undergone the necessary clinical trials. And, this untested shot could be authorized for children, who the CDC already recommends getting 29 doses of 9 other vaccines (plus a yearly flu shot after six months old) for kids aged 0 to 6 ("Vaccines" 2021), and that's only the shots they get up to 6 years old, and can be given to them, 5 at one time! If you look at the CDC immunization schedule up to 18 years of age, it is horrifying how many vaccines are put into children, and who knows what other novel viruses will require new shots deemed necessary under EUA, which keeps getting drawn out.

We also need to be very aware of dangerous bills, like SB 866, in California, allowing minors to get vaccinations, including Covid-19, without parental consent, which, thankfully, did not pass. Parents and lawyers, worked tirelessly for it to not go through, as well as, AB 1797, which mandates all of your medical vaccination status data to be entered into a government data base that you cannot opt out from. Those are just a few of the bills, but there will be more to come, no doubt, that will be equally concerning.

We really need to be aware of what we are experiencing on such a huge global scale, and how it set a whole new precedent for the way we will live in the days ahead. That is why being fully awake and aware is so crucial, to be able to navigate many more serious changes that will happen in the near future, and I can assure you they will truly make you feel that the rug has been pulled out from under you, especially if you were someone who went along with what you were told the whole time, and never questioned any of it. If ever there was a time to be fully awake, it is now!

Following the science, or following anything, for that matter, is not how we awaken. Unless, of course, you did "follow the science" and became skeptical and weary when the booster shots rolled out so quickly. Boosters are usually given when a vaccine wanes over time, but the Covid-19 experimental shot showed to be ineffective almost immediately, which is why the boosters were recommended so fast. One must ask how long that would keep going, especially since they want to get the Covid-19 shot on the immunization schedule for children, who are least likely to die from the virus. Or maybe you were on board to "follow the science" until you got injured, or someone you know got injured, and you realized that you have absolutely no recourse, whatsoever, to get help or compensation for your injury. I imagine that would wake you up out of anger, or even regret.

Keep in mind that when we were told to "follow the science", we were also told that the pharmaceutical industry was not liable for any injuries, if they were to happen. I'm still trying to make sense of how people were okay with that, on top of putting something in your body the pharmaceutical industry refuses to tell you what it is, and gets mandated to keep putting it in your body, again and again. Following the science means you're being asked to follow something experimental, so therefore potentially risky, and you should have complete faith and trust in, but then you are totally left on your own if anything bad were to happen to you. Doesn't seem like a fair exchange to me, but I guess when you are functioning out of fear, which most people were because we were blitzkrieged with fear 24/7, then I imagine some people would do anything to feel a sense of security, even if it was false.

Here's what I want you to know. Each one of us can awaken more, and if you're someone who feels that you weren't as awake and aware as you thought you were over the last few years, you are not alone. There are millions of people who went along with what they were told because they felt that they were doing the right thing, and I understand that. When you fear that you are facing a virus that can kill you, you can resort to all sorts of things that you think can help prevent that from happening.

But, let me ask you this. Was it a genuine fear of dying that influenced the decisions that you made during the pandemic, or that you believed you were going to die because you were "told" that you would, if you didn't go along with exactly what you were being told to do? Things like wearing a mask, social distancing, staying away from people; even loved ones, and harshly judging those that could be a threat to you because they chose not to put the Covid-19 experimental shot in their body, are all things we were told to do to stay safe.

As we now know, the Covid-19 experimental shot neither prevented getting the virus, or stopped it from spreading. You still might have your own personal beliefs around it, and that's fine. You can believe whatever you want to. But, please know that if you are judgmental of those who have different opinions or beliefs than you, or made different decisions for themselves because they believe in bodily autonomy, or subscribe to, "My body, my choice", just like that slogan is used for a woman to choose to give birth to her baby, or abort the fetus; the path of awakening is not likely for those who sit in judgment of others, and believe they are superior to those who think differently than they do.

The path of awakening is, as Victor Shamas says, something "we are all equally capable of" but not if we don't view each other as equal, and having a right to decide what is best for us. That cannot be determined by someone else, or an authority figure that we perceive as more powerful than us. We are powerful. And, we are free to determine that we are powerful without the control of others who claim they are more powerful under the guise of having authority over us. No one has agency over us, unless we allow them to.

For anyone who doesn't know this, we are in the midst

of a great (spiritual) awakening. If you thought this whole topsy-turvy period has just been about a virus, you are very mistaken. And, if you're someone who just wanted everything to return to "normal" so that life could go back to being what made you feel safe and secure, think again. What's safe about extreme censorship and cancel-culture? You may not agree with other's opinions that differ from yours, but if the government starts to police what they deem "misinformation", then free-speech will never be a right anyone of us can realize again. As George Washington said, "If freedom of speech is taken away, then dumb and silent we may be led, like sheep to the slaughter." The truth is, there is no one, or nothing that can stop us from knowing that we are powerful enough to resist anything that tries to control, censor, or destroy us. Not a government. Not a virus. Not a pandemic. The thing that is most destructive, and proposes the greatest threat to us is our ignorance. And, the only antidote for ignorance is having information or knowledge that we have a right to know.

And, who holds the key to information or knowledge?

We do.

Now let's use it to lead the way. We have a lot of work to do to awaken even more.

14

Are You Ready To Awaken?

You have to grow from the inside out.
None can teach you, none can make you spiritual.
There is no other teacher but your own soul.

- SWAMI VIVEKANANDA

The desire to awaken, or become more conscious, is something that has to come, as Swami Vivekananda says, "from the inside out", and it is our "soul" that needs to ignite us to want to know and encompass a wider sense of truth or reality.

It's curious why there are people who naturally gravitate towards a more spiritual, meaningful existence; and value learning and evolving on the life journey, and those that are more ego driven, and focus on materialism rather than spirituality. Spirituality involves exploring important themes like life and death, which some people are not comfortable looking at closely, and prefer avoiding those deeper subjects, as much as they can. If one has a true desire to grow, examining the more profound, existential topics of life is something that must be explored to come to know who we are beyond just our human, sensory experiences.

But not everyone has a desire to know more about who they are. They are fine or content knowing that they exist to exist, and their main focus is to keep their survival going for as long as they can, which brings me back to what I mentioned in the previous chapter about fear. When you fear death, you do all that you can to make sure that the possibility of death is nowhere near you. Not only is it a subject you don't prefer talking about, but your main objective is to stave off death at every turn. But, the truth is, death is not something we have total control over, even though we can do what we can to live safely, and keep ourselves out of harm's way, physically.

This brings me to mention, again, the last few years, where we were at the effect of every piece of doomsday news (thank you very much Anthony Fauci, CDC, and the World Health Organization), and the constant bombardment of the likelihood of dying from Covid-19, which was being driven into our minds; morning, noon and night. Death was not only a subject we couldn't avoid, we were fed daily the only way we could prevent dying was by taking the experimental Covid-19 shot, and if we didn't, we could kill those that did. I don't ever recall being told what healthy measures we could take to keep our immunity strong but instead, repeatedly told we were susceptible and vulnerable, and should not trust our own body's natural immune system. Many excellent and credible doctors whose careers were at risk for speaking out, like Dr. Peter McCullough, and Dr. Robert Malone (the inventor of the mRNA technology used for both the Moderna and Pfizer vaccines), spoke about the remarkable power of the body's natural immune system to fight illness, and pointed out that after contracting Covid-19, the body produces natural antibodies that give you plenty of immunity to not need the Covid-19 shot at all.

Even Brazil's President, Jair Bolsonaro, said he feels that "his immunity levels are through the roof", since having had the Covid-19 virus (Pedroso 2021), but the subject of our bodies natural immune system was never mentioned on the news during the entire pandemic.

I feel it's important to bring all of this up in order to be aware of what we've gone through, what have we learned from it, and what truth did we gather from it all. I don't think that you can be ready to awaken unless you are open to discussing what all of us have gone through over the last few years. It has been extremely stressful, and for many, they don't feel that they've recovered from it, not just physically, if you've had Covid, but emotionally and psychologically.

It's been very challenging, and the purpose of this book is to awaken us to what we have been through, to make us more aware, conscious human beings. If we don't look at the deeper themes of human existence, like death, and explore our relationship to this natural occurrence of the life cycle, then we really can't understand how to handle or navigate extremely demanding situations we find ourselves in. Things like a major health crisis, or a pandemic (also called *Plandemic* — the name of film maker and author, Mikki Willis' book, and film, which is the most seen and censored documentary in history), will continue to cause us to function out of fear.

I'm sure this is just the beginning of future situations – new viruses, and pandemics, or "plandemics", if you subscribe to the belief that people like "Dr. Anthony Fauci, Bill Gates, and organizations like the CDC, NIH, WHO, and Bill & Melinda Gates Foundation, among others", are "driving the global vaccination agenda", and there are "tech giant and mainstream media forces doing their utmost to silence and suppress the veracity of these findings", as Mikki Willis believes and writes about in his book, *Plandemic* (Plandemic 2021). All of this will test our strength and resiliency, and if we haven't learned from this recent pandemic how to be more awake, aware, and conscious human beings, then we will carry over a collective unconsciousness into challenging, or life-threatening events in the future. There was tremendous polarization during this difficult time, and I feel that it was stirred up by the media. You have to be very awake and aware to see the ways in which we are being manipulated by the media for reasons that are highly questionable. Having an awareness of how the media exploits and manipulates us is a perfect example of how the term "conspiracy theory" gets propagated. The sheer mentioning of propaganda and the media raises eyebrows amongst those that watch the news like they're listening to a Sunday church sermon. People have quoted, verbatim, what they've heard back to me, as if they're reading from a news teleprompter. I find that alarming, and an indication that groupthink was at work, rather than using individual critical thinking skills.

So, my question to you now is, do you feel that you are ready to awaken to what's really going on, so that you can know and encompass a wider sense of truth and reality? Look, I'm not going to pretend that the path of awakening is an easy one, or isn't uncomfortable at times to be on. It's not pleasant to see what's really going on, or accept that people in positions of power, and even our government, or health organizations, can tell us things that aren't necessarily true. As a matter of fact, at times they could be flat out lying to us, which I have no doubt we were lied to on many occasions during the last few years about the pandemic. I can imagine some of you thinking, "I don't believe that!", or again, "Why would they do that to us?!" Well, you need to do your own deep dive into these areas that go way beyond just what you're being told. All you have to do is revisit some of the blatant contradictions or mixed messages we received from

our government, the WHO, the CDC, big pharma, and
Anthony Fauci, who never once mentioned something
like taking vitamin C, D, Zinc, or Glutathione, "which
is the most powerful and potent antioxidant that detoxi-
fies the entire body" ("Glutathione" n.d), or other helpful
therapeutics to get through Covid-19. As the Director
of NIAID (National Institute of Allergy and Infectious
Diseases), Fauci does oversee research to prevent, diag-
nose, and "treat" infectious diseases, after-all. If anything,
he single-handedly debunked the effectiveness of a drug
that's been around since the late 1970's called Ivermectin, and has "led many to describe it as a wonder drug"
(Crump and Ōmura 2011). Many doctors used Ivermectin as part of their protocol for treating Covid-19 with
very positive results, even though they were admonished
by their superiors not to (doctors take the Hippocrat-
ic Oath, which is an oath of ethics where the physician
pledges to prescribe only beneficial treatments, so where
did this order come from to stop giving patients Ivermectin, which was beneficial?) Dr. Simone Gold (founder of
America's Frontline Doctors), spoke about the benefits of
Ivermectin, and how she was admonished by her superiors
to give it to her patients. The YouTube video went viral
with over a million views, but was taken down because of
censorship. And, Dr. Vladamir Zelenko, a globally, well-
known researcher, and Nobel Peace Prize Appointee, gave
his patients Ivermectin as part of his Covid-19 treatment
protocol, which he believed saved lives. Both of these

excellent doctors, who acted more like medical human-
itarians, were heavily censored, due to this extreme cancel-culture. We need to know the truth about why Fauci
"implored" people to stop taking Ivermectin, which he
called a "horse de-wormer" (Baragona 2021). This made
people wary of Ivermectin's efficacy for humans, and it
soon became almost impossible to get. I suggest you ask
why he was encouraging, instead, to use the drug, Remdesivir, which causes "nausea, constipation, pain, bleeding,
bruising of the skin, soreness or swelling near where the
medication was injected, renal dysfunction, and possible
liver and kidney dysfunction."

There are so many dubious things about Anthony Fauci — his ties to the pharmaceutical industry, the
Wuhan Lab, and "Gain-of-function research", to name
a few. I highly recommend reading Robert F. Kennedy
Jr.'s excellent, jaw-dropping book, *The Real Anthony Fauci*,
which is one of the best, well researched biographies out
there (you can watch the movie directed by Jeff Hays at
Childrenshealthdefense.org). The media has done everything they can to vilify Robert, and discredit him and
his book, which is another example of censorship and
cancel-culture at work on a massive scale. It would have
been extremely helpful (and life-saving) to have a team of
top doctors, other than just Fauci, weighing in on how we
could have stayed healthy, and naturally boosted our immune system during the Covid-19 outbreak, other than

just listening to him contradict himself on far too many occasions. There is a video of him from 2004 which has gone viral on social media, where he said about a woman who had the flu that she didn't need to get the flu shot because, "The most potent vaccination is getting infected (with the virus) yourself, and you're as protected as anybody" ("User Clip: Fauci on Natural Immunity Being Most Potent Vaccine 2004 | C-SPAN.org" n.d.).

When he's questioned by Senator Rand Paul in a Senate Health Committee hearing in 2022, he asks Fauci, "Why did he embrace basic immunology back in 2004, and reject it now?" Fauci defends himself by reading something from Reuters, which completely contradicts his earlier stance on natural immunity. Rand Paul's answer speaks volumes when he says to him, "words don't lie" (Rand Paul Confronts Fauci with Video of His Own Past Statements on Natural Immunity" n.d.). How convenient (and curious) of Fauci to recently step down as the head of the NIAID. I have no doubt he will be questioned more, or legally charged for, not only his Gain-of-Function Wuhan Lab research (Browne 2021), but how he misled the American people, causing unnecessary injuries and deaths, which could have been avoided.

Please do your own research, and don't continue to rely on being told the truth by others who might have a secret, even sinister agenda you know nothing about. This might sound conspiracy-theory(ish) to you, and if you feel that way, you need to put that highly manipulative, and divisive term aside. If you're a questioner, and want to know the truth, you're going to have to work a little bit harder to find it, and if you don't want to do that, then I don't think you should inconvenience yourself by putting yourself on the path of awakening. Unless you are ready to accept that *The Wizard of Oz* was just a little old man hiding behind a curtain, and frightening poor little Dorothy, Toto, and her sweet friends; who were all in search of something they desperately needed (brain, a heart, and courage), maybe there's something you need, that keeps you stuck in believing that people in power, (Fauci, the government, the pharmaceutical industry, the WHO, the CDC, The NIH, and the FDA), are infallible, or beyond reproach.

Again, if the pharmaceutical industry really did care about us, why are they completely off the hook if you get injured by the Covid-19 shot, or any other vaccine, for that matter? There's a lot more names to add to that group that people think walk on water, but as it's been said, "Follow the money, and you will know who's in control."

So, again, I ask you, do you feel that you are ready to awaken? If your answer is yes, I commend you for being a seeker of truth. We need you on our truth-seeking mission to turn this ship around before it turns into a global Titanic. I believe it is the seekers of truth who will inherit this earth, not the meek, as it is said in Psalms 37:11.

This is not the time to be "meek," or asleep.

CHAPTER 3

What You Need To Know About Awakening

The universe has shaken you to awaken you.

- ANONYMOUS

If you feel that you have begun, or are in the midst of a spiritual awakening, you should consider yourself lucky. Not everyone gets a chance to emerge from what I call a "sleepwalker trance", and find themselves in a conscious state of lucid truth. It's like taking off a pair of dark glasses to keep the sun out, and realize that you never needed to shield yourself from the light, your vision just needed to get stronger to handle its radiance. It's actually not natural to wear sunglasses that much, and studies show that it can interfere with our circadian rhythm, which can lead to fatigue, insomnia, and even depression, but how would we know that, if that hasn't been told to us, and just assume it's natural for us to wear them, and we do, for long periods of time.

We go along with so many things that are unnatural, and accept them as normal, and before we know it, we've conformed to certain ways of living because it's expected of us to do so, and what's considered normal is not questioned. Does that mean that when the world turns completely upside down because of a "pandemic", and we're told that this is the "new normal", and we should get used to living in a perpetual "state of emergency" that can cause us to feel like yo-yo's; never knowing when we'll have to go into lockdown (again), or have to mask ourselves, and practice social distancing, or get, yet again, another booster (and who knows what else we'll be told to do), we should just go along with it?

It is completely unnatural to be in a constant state of fear of viral contamination. We have been living with viruses since the beginning of time, so why would we allow this particular virus to keep us in a state of fear that seems never ending. Again, be mindful of asking questions because once you readily accept what is being told to you, you allow yourself to be controlled by those who will tell you what they think is best for you to stay alive, and before you know it, you will find yourself doing things that literally defy logic, and not even know that you are. Hopefully, after seeing the president of the United States get Covid after two shots, and two boosters, you remember that he said in 2021, "You're not going to get Covid if you have these vaccinations", ("Joe Biden Gets COVID " n.d.), and are now seriously questioning the logic around putting an experimental shot in your body that does not protect you from Covid, nor stop the transmission of it.

If you remain in an unnatural state of constant fear, you will become less aware of what's actually causing it because you're in a fight or flight response, and easily triggered to flee from what could harm you, which we have been told incessantly is the Covid-19 virus. This makes you function like some kind of animal who is always on the lookout for its predator, and also explains why people who believed they were protected by the Covid shot, turned on those who chose not to take it, and perceived them as the greatest threat to their survival. You would think there would have been more people using critical thinking skills to question those in positions of power or authority, and see if what they were saying actually made total sense. Rather than just giving into being told we should be very afraid of a novel virus that came from a bat, maybe we should have insisted on more evidence to prove, if, in fact, that was true. I do have to remind myself that millions of people chose to get injected with an experimental shot without informed consent, "a principal in medical ethics and medical law that a patient should have sufficient information before making their own free

decisions about their medical care" (American Medical
Association 2016), so they are not going to be the ones
who need "sufficient information", let alone, more evidence to prove that what is being told to them is true.
Bottom line is, when you are functioning out of fear, all
you care about is staying alive, so logic is the last thing
you're concerned about. But, for someone who is awake,
that's the first thing they take into consideration, and ask
themselves something like, "Is my thinking sound", or
"Am I being reactive?" They are not a slave to fear, or live
each moment preoccupied with their survival. An awake
person is much deeper than that, and when awake people
talk to each other, it's not about how they can stay alive
out of desperation, but more about sharing ideas of how
to live more consciously, which includes living healthy
and wholesomely, so they can be happy human beings;
mind, body, and spirit.

Let me ask you a question. If you had a lot of fear
during the pandemic, don't you think it would have been
wiser to decide, first, if you should just automatically go
into fear because you were told to be afraid, or instead,
think for yourself if you want to go into fear mode? You
may not know that fear is something we can actually elect
to accept, or reject, and a very good way to do that is to
listen very carefully to what is being told to you, and look
at the evidence that is being presented (provable evidence
must be presented, as should informed consent so a person

or patient has sufficient information before making their own decisions about their medical care, which means the possible risks of what they are taking), and decide if it adds up, or rings true for you. And, if it doesn't, logic prevails, and you simply don't allow yourself to succumb to an emotion like fear because you are being told to.

That is being awake, and not a sleepwalker. Being a sleepwalker isn't something I think people consciously decide for themselves, but, sadly, can happen to anyone who just isn't awake enough to know that they are not as fully conscious and aware as they can be. What's scary about that, is you can be so unconscious about something that is extremely important to know, that you are actually functioning like someone who is sleepwalking through your life. I recommend watching the movie, *Invasion of the Body Snatchers*, which is about how people are being replaced by emotionless imposters, and alien species of human duplicates are taking over a small town. It might seem odd to mention a movie like that, but I think it's very appropriate for the times we are in, since, like the movie, people didn't believe what was happening to them until there were only two survivors left to destroy the pod people (a species of plant-like aliens).

I'm hopeful that as more people awaken, we won't wait, but instead, take-action against anyone or anything that wants to mislead, and possibly destroy us.

28

Waking Up To A Virtual Reality And Transhumanism

Virtual reality was once the dream of science fiction. But the internet was also once a dream, and so were computers and smartphones. The future is coming.

- MARK ZUCKERBERG

Most people are awaiting Virtual Reality. I'm awaiting virtuous reality.

- ELI KHAMAROV

This brings me to another thing that has become a part of our "new normal", and that's Facebook's "Metaverse". Mark Zuckerberg seems to perceive this universe as quite imperfect, and felt the need to create a virtual world he believes is far more superior to this one. Instead of taking responsibility for a planet we continue to destroy, it's just so easy to create a virtual world that is better than the real one, and all we have to do is have an avatar (computer representation of yourself), and let it live out our reality for us. Personally, I have zero interest in wearing a VR (virtual reality) headset to be in another reality that my avatar lives in. The whole thing is creepy, and rather nauseating, which also happens to be a common side effect people complain about when wearing the VR headsets; nausea.

I can assure you that when you experience a spiritual awakening, nausea is the last thing you will feel. Feelings of inner peace, wholeness, oneness; even bliss or euphoria, have been some of the descriptions of going through a spiritual awakening. Why anyone would prefer nausea over bliss is beyond me, but one of my theories about people who avoid spirituality, or anything that makes them feel more than what they are comfortable with, is that they are choosing to avoid a state of consciousness they perceive as uncontrollable, and being in something like the Metaverse, you can be in control of everything, including your emotions, or lack thereof.

In the awakening process, you will begin to notice how we are dehumanizing ourselves by devaluing things like real human emotions. Not only are we creating virtual versions of ourselves, but we actually began this process long ago by anesthetizing our feelings with pharmaceutical drugs (and that's why we should trust big pharma?) So, we learn to numb ourselves to cope with real feelings; be it of pain or sorrow, which is a natural part of the human condition, and now are being invited to go into a virtual reality where we are numb, or dead emotionally, which is perfect in an emotion-free simulated world. Does this not disturb you? It should.

Another thing you might be completely unaware of is this movement towards Transhumanism, which is "The belief or theory that the human race can evolve beyond its current physical and mental limitations, especially by means of science and technology" (Gleiser 2014).

Yes, we as human beings have physical and mental limitations, but does that mean we should become avatars, or even robots to rid ourselves of these "limitations?" Another definition of transhumanism is, "A philosophical and intellectual movement which advocates for the enhancement of the human condition by developing and making widely available and sophisticated technologies that can greatly enhance longevity and cognition" (Wikipedia Contributors 2019). Here we are trying to "enhance longevity and cognition" for as long as we possibly can, but at what expense? I mean, I guess we all want to live for as long as we possibly can, but it seems to me that this philosophy is more about extending life by avoiding death, and doing what we can with "science and technology" to make that happen. If the goal of transhumanism is to "encourage the use of bio-transformative technologies in order to enhance the human organism, with the ultimate aim being to modify the human organism so radically as to overcome fundamental human limitations" (Transhumanist FAQ 2016), then we are on a very fast-moving trajectory for that to happen. And, when we hear about things like "microchipping" people, which apparently has already begun in "techno-forward Sweden", it seems to confirm that we are well on our way to becoming more like computers than humans.

According to an article in USA Today on August 1, 2020, they cite a claim that "all Americans will receive a microchip implant by the end of the year" (Caldera 2020), which was taken from a viral article from the website "My Healthy Life Guru." They quote from that article, "Some people are concerned that the federal government will be very influential with this revolutionized RFID Microchip. They could see every move we make," the article warns, and "your food and money will be also managed with these microchips." This all sounds like some sci-fi thriller, don't you think? We may not be microchipped by the end of the year, but it's already being implemented, which means that it's only a matter of time before it will be presented to all of us. And, being that president Biden recently signed a "China competition bill" (Breuninger 2022) "to boost US microchip makers" (DeMattia 2022) and sent "53 billion to US chipmakers" ("Biden Signs CHIPS Act" 2022), we're going to be very well prepared, and "lead the world in the production of these chips for our own safety's sake, as well as our economic growth", as Biden said (DeMattia 2022). If microchipping is already being talked about for human use (our animals were a prelude), according to an article in AfroTech, "Elon Musk will reportedly be implanting microchips into humans as early as this year" (Dorisca 2022), it does seem like microchipping humans is in the works for our not-too-distant future. In the article, it says that "Musk shared with the Wall Street Journal's CEO Council Summit what's to come with Neuralink", which is the brain interface technology company he co-founded in 2016. The article also says that, "the implant has already been tested on a monkey who was featured playing MindPong."

Let me just say, for anyone who finds something like a spiritual awakening boring compared to a microchipped monkey playing MindPong, or "being at one" with your computer and 5G technology, which promises to make significant improvements in virtual and augmented reality, maybe this has become your substitute for God, and you might think, "Who needs God when you can be God" and control your destiny by creating the exact type of (microchipped) universe you want, which transcends (human) mental and physical limitations?

The whole idea of humans being microchipped, is probably quite alluring for transhumanists who believe we have outgrown any limitation that keeps us stuck in "samsara", which is a Buddhist term that means, "the cycle of death and rebirth to which life in the material world is bound." For us to transcend this material world we are bound, we need to evolve spiritually. That means we must do the inner work it requires to not live and act like animals so that we can raise our consciousness to higher levels of awareness. To think that we can bypass this and use "science and technology" to be in a virtual world, or blast us right off this earth onto another planet we think will be better than this one, is the biggest cop-out of our humanity, in my opinion. Rather than taking full responsibility for how we are single handedly destroying this great planet, and want to trans-humanize ourselves, is shameful. And, for those of us who value this earth, and recognize our purpose here as light-workers (conscious human beings), we are truly horrified by how many people want the fast, drive-through version of existence, and will do whatever they can to keep themselves alive at all costs. These types of people fear death, and are dragging the rest of us into their fear, which could destroy us all, and this planet.

To think that so many people who believed in bodily autonomy, and didn't want to take the Covid-19 experimental shot, were perceived as selfish by those who couldn't roll their sleeves up fast enough to get it (without knowing what's in it), and went along with Bill Gates (a computer software developer who has become the arbiter of our health), is very troubling. They thought anyone who had a mind of their own was selfish, but maybe avoiding doing the work you need to do to truly wake up, is the greatest act of selfishness there is. Here's what you need to know about awakening. You cannot be selfish, and only think of yourself. You must include your fellow man, woman, and child, and respect whatever decisions they make for themselves. We are not put on this earth just to have everyone go along with our opinions and beliefs. We are here on this earth to co-exist, and evolve while we are here, which means evolve this planet with us, not destroy it.

If one does not make a conscious effort to awaken and evolve, they are contributing to the destruction of this earth. And, if you think that transcending our humanism and becoming more machine like is how we need to evolve, then you are functioning as a transhumanist, and I would be very wary of anyone who is showing signs that they are. People like Elon Musk, Mark Zuckerberg, Bill Gates, and Klaus Schwab (German engineer, and founder and president of the World Economic Forum, WEF, which consists of some of the wealthiest people in the world, also referred to as "global elites", who are in great positions of power), are those you need to know about, and what their agendas are. They (and plenty of others; again please do your research), want us to live exactly as they dictate, and have control over you, if you allow it.

Do not wait until it's too late to wake up to what is happening right before your eyes. Remember, each of us holds the key to information and knowledge. If you are someone who doesn't want to know more, then you are choosing to stay asleep, and when the world has changed radically, which it already has during the pandemic, you will be clueless, until you too, have your freedom(s) taken from you, one by one, and no one will be able to protect you from that. Please wake up, and join the awakened ones as we create Our New World, and resist the "New World Order", which is a tyrannical world governance "reset" led by Klaus Schwab, and the global elites of the international business world, who, by the way, fly their private jets to the Davos climate change conference (are you not seeing what's "really" going on?"). Keep in mind that if you research what is truly behind the New World Order (NWO), it will probably be referred to as mostly conspiracy theories, which is not at all surprising. I also want to mention that it makes me very uncomfortable to have discovered, while researching Klaus Schwab, there are rumors that his father, Eugene, was a close confident of Adolf Hitler, and also a manager of a Swiss-German Nazi company (Adl-Tabatabai 2022). There are articles that claim this rumor about Schwab's father is a conspiracy theory, but also articles that say it's true. Again, do your own research, and dig as deep as you can until you get answers that sit right with you. It is incumbent upon each one of us who want to know the actual truth, to make it our business to find it, even if that means spending countless hours watching, or listening to whatever you can find. I recommend videos or podcasts like rfkjrpodcast, with Robert F. Kennedy, Jr., subscribing to Children's Health Defense newsletter, and CHD.TV, ICAN (Informed Consent Network) with Del Bigtree, Daily Clout with Naomi Wolf, The Stew Peters Show on BrighteonTV, Breitbart News Network with Steve Bannon, The Epoch Times and EpochTV, America's Frontline Doctors News, Dr. Robert Malone's newsletter at rwmalone.substack. com, The McCullough Report on Apple Podcasts with Dr. Peter McCullough, and Dr. Mercola, mercola.com, (there are too many to list all). There are so many excellent doctors, scientists, and thought leaders, you probably never heard of during the pandemic because they were heavily censored, but deserve being listened to, and taken very seriously.

The truth cannot be determined for us by anyone else, especially those you assume are telling you the truth because they are in a position of authority. And, truth shouldn't feel as if it's being forced upon you, or you're being coerced to buy into it. I was very skeptical about how many ways the government was coercing people into getting the Covid-19 experimental shot, the most desperate — giving away free Krispy Kreme donuts, which are anything but healthy! And remember, someone who is in a position of authority, could be quick to call you a conspiracy theorist, if you question them.

Please keep in mind what Benjamin Franklin said:

"It is the first responsibility of every citizen to question authority."

CHAPTER 5

Why Awakening Is So Important Right Now

Ego implies unawareness.
Unawareness and ego cannot coexist.

- ECKHART TOLLE

Awakening, and becoming more conscious, is extremely important at any time in life, but especially right now. After two years of a global pandemic, everything has changed radically because of it. Here are some of the major changes it has caused:

1. There has been a precipitous decline in mental health. Millions of people have experienced depression, a decline in their physical health, and have an overall feeling of hopelessness and despair.

2. There has been a deep impact on society and politics. Many people perceive that our government and political culture has degraded over the course of the pandemic. Politicians are fighting constantly, and are polarized more than ever, which is causing a greater polarization amongst people, creating dissent and chaos in society. Many people fear that the republic of the United States is ending, and what will come next is autocracy, fascism, and civil war.

3. The economy has tanked, and far too many businesses have shut down (while liquor stores remained open the entire time during the pandemic), and yet, California Governor, Gavin Newsom, claimed that he spent over a billion of our tax dollars on masks from China, and our government is apparently giving $75 million of our tax dollars to illegal aliens.

4. Work-life has disappeared for millions of people. The pandemic has greatly impacted the decline of jobs, disrupting the careers of those who either lost their jobs, or had their work reduced to the point where they are having serious financial difficulties, causing tremendous stress and uncertainty.

5. Remote working is quickly replacing in-person employment, and many people are having a hard time going back to the workplace. Although some people welcome the change, others find it more isolating, and feel anxious about the possibility of returning to a physical work environment.

6. There has been a tremendous impact on relationships. The pandemic created intense polarization amongst family, friends, and marriages, causing people to fight over Covid-19 vaccine opinions and beliefs, which erupted into a "vaxed/ anti-vax" frenzy, stoked by the government's mandates, "anti-vax" narratives, and the politicization of health. Relationships have ended because of it, and many feel estranged and ostracized from loved ones.

7. There is an alarming increase in pharmaceuticals. Having lived in fear for two years, people are having a very hard time shaking it off, especially when there is constant talk about the "next variant" coming. Medications used for anxiety, depression and sleep disruption are at an all-time high, and suicide has increased at an alarming rate.

8. The slogan: "We are all in this together" has actually turned into "We are further apart." People feel more divided than ever, and based on what we see (that isn't censored) there is a deep divide amongst people who choose to go along with whatever Covid narrative they believe in, and those who oppose it. Instead of getting along, and co-existing mindfully, there is an overall sense of barely tolerating each other's differences, rather than learning more about how to understand and embrace them.

9. There is an overwhelming fear of the future. Millions of people feel that there is a lack in leadership, and don't trust government to guide us effectively, or safely at

a time of great uncertainty. This has caused an erosion of trust in scientists, doctors, and health officials, creating what feels like an even stronger chokehold by the government and health officials to control people's decisions regarding their health. With the recent amendments being made to the International Health Regulations, the WHO director-general, Dr. Tedros, could be the man deciding if our countries are facing a "public health threat", and with the new pandemic treaty coming up, the WHO will also be deciding how our countries should respond to it, which means they are in complete control of whatever health protocols they deem necessary, even if we choose not to agree, or go along with it. There is no way of knowing what kind of consequences we can face if we stand up for bodily autonomy, or defending our rights for medical freedom.

10. Is tyranny the "new normal"? Many people feel that there are dictators running their country, as well as medical and pharmaceutical elites controlling our health, and violating our HIPPA privacy laws by forcing us to disclose our medical decisions and history. Our civil liberties are being stripped and denied over a virus that still remains a mystery about its origins, and the FDA says "it will take the agency 55 years to answer a Freedom of Information Act (FOIA) request for extensive vaccine data and transparency about the Pfizer Covid-19 vaccine" (Greene 2021). Manipulating people with fear, which our

government and health organizations have done so well, has left people feeling overwhelmingly fearful, therefore more susceptible to being controlled and manipulated, as we fight for our freedoms that are quickly being taken from us.

All of this (and there's more) should explain why we must awaken at a time when, if we don't, we will succumb to a type of global tyranny, of which we have not seen in our lifetime (New World Order, which means global governance). You must realize that it is our ego that keeps us stuck in denial and ignorance because it is far too important for us to hold onto a personal ideology that serves our needs, as I mentioned, for survival. As Joseph Heller said in *Catch-22*, "The enemy is anybody who's going to get you killed, no matter which side he is on." So, depending on which side you are on, be it political, medical, philosophical, religious, or existential, you will side with whoever supports your need to stay alive, and how you choose to do it. But, what if the very person or thing that you believe will keep you safe and alive, is, in fact, your enemy, but you just don't know it? Are you 100% certain that everything you believe will keep you safe and alive, actually will? How is it possible that everything that you experienced in the last two years of the pandemic, made complete sense to you, and there was absolutely nothing about the way it was handled that didn't make sense, even a little bit, but maybe it's too hard to admit it?

Please, just stay with me on this. You tell me how the Covid-19 virus can know exactly what you're doing, and how, when you were eating in a restaurant, you could take off the mask (the virus is giving you a break), but when you were walking to the bathroom for less than a minute, it was required to wear a mask. The same can be said about taking off the mask while eating pretzels on a plane, but forced to wear a mask the remainder of the flight (when I say "forced", I literally mean that you would be forced off the plane if you did not comply). Or, how do you feel now knowing that all of those packages you cleaned with some kind of anti-bacterial wipe or spray during the lockdown, was told to you by the WHO that it really wasn't necessary to do, after-all, because the virus can't live on surfaces, and is air-born. Doesn't that annoy you now, just a little bit? Or, how about California mayor, Eric Garcetti going to a football game with 70,000 people, and was seen mask-less, but claimed it was okay because he held his breath when his mask was off. Please admit that was a ludicrous thing to say! Do these people really think we are that stupid? And then, as we know, Governor Newsom was spotted at the French Laundry restaurant at the height of the pandemic when Covid was supposedly most contagious, and Speaker of the United States House of Representatives, Nancy Pelosi, was spotted at her hair salon mask-less, but that was okay because, clearly, they live by the edict, "Rules for thee, but not for me."

What more will it take for you to realize that waking up is the very thing that will actually keep you alive, not to mention, sane, and if you choose to not want to see or know the truth, it may very well be your undoing? I don't care if you're a doctor, lawyer, or a government official, if you can't question your own beliefs, no matter the top education or degrees you have, because it's just too threatening to do so, and causes you to second guess everything you have believed your entire adult (or professional) life, you need to know that this is a time to question everything, for that is the only way you can truly awaken in a world that feels as if it has gone into what Dr. Robert Malone has called, "mass formation psychosis". Psychology professor, Mattias Desmet, PhD, who developed the theory, writes more about it in his book, *The Psychology of Totalitarianism*. In it, he says, "Mass formation is, in essence, a kind of group hypnosis that destroys individuals' ethical self-awareness and robs them of their ability to think clearly. This process is insidious in nature; populations fall prey to it unsuspectingly." He quotes Yuval Noah Harari (who happens to be a lead advisor to World Economic Forum founder, Klaus Schwab) saying, "Most people wouldn't even notice the shift toward a totalitarian regime. We associate totalitarianism mainly with labor, concentration, and extermination camps, but those are merely the final, bewildering stage of a long process." By the way, mass formation psychosis, is also being called a conspiracy theory term. Based on what Harari is saying, would we call "mass formation psychosis" a conspiracy theory if it was used to describe the mental state people were in when they did get to the final stage that resulted in the Holocaust?

It's time to awaken, my friend, and I hope that you agree. After all, what do you have to lose by waking up a little more? Discovering something that can make you feel more knowledgeable, and therefore more empowered? Is that such a bad thing? Or is it that you just prefer being led, rather than leading yourself, so that you needn't take responsibility for the decisions you make, and if they prove to be wrong, you won't have to blame yourself for making them? And, even if you entrusted others to make important decisions for you, and now realize that perhaps some of them have been misleading, or wrong, are you able to admit that to yourself? Or, is it too ego-sensitive to admit that you allowed others to make some of the most important decisions of your life for you; one of those decisions, to put something in your body like the Covid-19 experimental shot that you have absolutely no way of knowing what effect it will have on you and your health in the future, and maybe the "powers that be" didn't tell you the "entire" truth about it, and now you must admit to yourself that you gave your power away because you were too afraid to trust yourself? If that's the case, please forgive yourself for it. We all have made decisions we wish we hadn't because we were either too afraid, insecure, uncertain, doubtful, pressured, or just felt more comfortable doing what others were doing, and lacked the courage at the time to stand up to what we were being told, even though we knew in our hearts that something just didn't feel right, but were too scared to act alone, and walk the intrepid path of a truth-seeker.

Here's a quote I want to share with you about being a truth-seeker:

"If you seek truth you will not seek victory by dishonorable means, and if you find truth you will become invincible."

– Epictetus

Why Ignorance Is Not Bliss

If ignorance is bliss, why aren't more people happy?

- THOMAS JEFFERSON

I had mentioned earlier that the greatest threat to us is our ignorance, and I'll take it one step farther with political activist and writer, Emma Goldman's quote, "The most violent element in society is ignorance."

A lack of knowledge or information can actually be dangerous, which is why ignorance is something we should pay close attention to, whether it's our own lack of awareness, or others. The problem is that when we are not self-aware, we don't know what we don't know until something makes us aware of it, and sometimes it can be too late. And, most people probably wouldn't want to know what they're unaware of because they think, as the saying goes, that "ignorance is bliss", which it most definitely is not. Ignorance is only bliss to those who prefer ignorance over taking responsibility for more than perhaps they want to know, which might be things that are unpleasant, and could upset their perfect little world where no problems exist.

When you choose to remain ignorant, you are free from what you don't know, so therefore don't have to worry about what doesn't concern or pertain to you. But, if we put that in a present day context, there is so much to be concerned about, if you're choosing to tune out, or simply don't want to know about what's going on in all of the areas I've discussed so far, like the many complex layers to the Covid-19 pandemic, and how it's been, and continues to be handled all over the world, which appears to be in a tyrannical manner, especially in countries like Canada and Australia, and, of course, China, then what you think doesn't pertain to you, actually does, but you just don't know it, yet. I don't have a crystal ball, and cannot see the future, but what I try to do, is pay very close attention to what I see and hear, and as I suggested to you in an earlier chapter about it being incumbent upon all of us to get the information that we need, to make us more knowledge-able about what's really going on in the world, and what could possibly happen in the future, I can say with cer-tainty that the world has changed radically, and it's only just beginning.

There are many theories about what's coming down the pike, but I don't want to go by theories, or focus on what "could" or "might" happen. But, as I mentioned earlier, hearing about the recent amendments being made to the International Health Regulations, and the WHO's director-general, Dr. Tedros, being the man who can singlehandedly decide if our countries are facing a public health threat, is very concerning. I suggest you check his political background, and not just his education – read "Dr. Cover-up: Tedros Adhanom's controversial journey to the WHO" (Goel 2020). And, as I also said, with the new pandemic treaty coming up, and the WHO deciding how countries should respond to it, which means they are in complete control of whatever health protocols they deem necessary, even if we choose not to agree, or go along with it, would threaten our bodily autonomy, and our medical freedom, as we've known it, will be taken from us, and possibly never return.

I want to point out that even if you're fine with the government, or health organizations making decisions for you about your health, if at any time you change your mind and decide that you don't want to go along with what they're mandating, or you or someone you know has been injured by a vaccine, you won't be able to. You, along with millions of other people, who already decided that mandating what we should put in our bodies against our

will, or without informed consent, is completely uncon-
stitutional, will have absolutely no say in the matter. And,
like we saw during the pandemic, if you did not comply
with the mandates, you were unable to enjoy your life
the way you would like to, let alone work, and I have no
doubt that it could happen all over again if Dr. Tedros decides we are facing another "public health threat." People
couldn't even go to places of worship during the pandemic, visit a loved one in a nursing home, and most heart-
breaking, attend a funeral of a family member during that
time, but as I pointed out, liquor stores remained open the
entire time. I don't think you should be ignorant about
that. No, I think you should be anything but ignorant to
the very strange things that are going on right in front of
our eyes. Decisions are being made for us like we are children who are incapable of making decisions for ourselves.
And, we're not allowed to voice our opinions about the
decisions that are being made for us by our government
and health organizations, or else we run the risk of being
censored or cancelled.

I'm on social media, and have been shocked by how
many people have been completely unaware of the extreme amount of censorship and cancel culture that's
going on right now. Again, that goes back to if it doesn't
pertain to you, then you don't have to know, or care about
it. You'd have to be living under a rock not to know how
many people have been censored, cancelled, or vilified

about speaking out during the last two years. I happen to know Robert F. Kennedy Jr., and when he was taken off Instagram and de-platformed, I was outraged. I found what he was posting on Instagram during the pandemic extremely helpful, and I was able to get information I found informative (even though the fact checkers, whoever they are, call anything that opposes or disrupts the "unquestionable" narrative, "misinformation"). Robert is not "anti-vax", but because he has tried to help those who have been vaccine injured, they ruthlessly try to vilify him, and besmirch his reputation again and again. The hostility toward those who are speaking the truth is frightening, and has provoked a type of anger in people that at times has felt that it could easily erupt into violence. It makes you wonder why we haven't heard our own government, or health officials discourage hostility at a time when there is so much polarization, but instead, go after people who they say are spreading "misinformation", when so many of them, like Robert F. Kennedy Jr. are genuinely trying to help people. They've even gone so far as singling out a group of people, including Kennedy, who have shared helpful information, and calling them the "Disinformation Dozen" (Sinsabaugh, Annie and Chakrabarti 2021), which has become a type of modern-day witch hunt. Both Facebook and Twitter have suspended some of their accounts, or required them to delete their posts or tweets.

Ignorance at a time like this can only be compared to Nazi Germany, in my opinion. For anyone who takes offense by this comparison, please listen to Holocaust survivor, activist, and founder of the Alliance for Human Research Protection, Vera Shirav ("Activist Vera Shiraz thought 'the WAR against Humanity' Told by a Holocaust Survivor n.d.), who has likened these times to Nazi Germany because of our silence and passivity in the face of tyranny and censorship. We should be on high alert to anything that even slightly resembles behaviors like government overreach or oppressive rule. If we learned anything about the horrors and atrocities that took place in Nazi Germany, it is that we should never stand idly by when we hear or see anything that could violate our rights, freedoms, and civil liberties, which is already happening. "Never again", is a Holocaust phrase that means we must never let what happened in Nazi Germany happen again. In order for history not to repeat itself means that we have learned our greatest lessons from it, but if we remain ignorant to what is happening right under our noses, and collude to deny it, we are doomed to repeat our transgressions again, and all shall suffer because of it.

Yes, ignorance is "the most violent element in society."

CHAPTER 7

Understanding Our Fears

Courage is knowing what not to fear.

- PLATO

To have a true awakening, one must face their fears. We cannot come to know who we are, unless we are willing to go into the depths of our being, and find out what is most frightening to us. It is in the knowing of our fears, we can face them, understand them, and overcome them, but if we don't, we will bury our fears somewhere deep within us, and do all that we can to make sure they are kept under tight control. If that is the case, you will go through life needing to be in control of as much as you possibly can, and when life throws you a curveball, you will try to control your world even more by accepting whatever is presented to you by people in positions of authority, believing they are genuinely helping to control your world with you, or even for you, which you will gladly welcome.

That is why when we are faced with a crisis, or most recently, a pandemic, and we haven't confronted our greatest fears, we can easily believe what is told to us by people we deem as authorities, or experts, and if we do exactly as we are told by them, everything is going to be fine. When you rely on others to manage, or assuage your worst fears, you are willingly at the mercy of everything they tell you to do, which could mean that you would do pretty much anything they suggest, even if it is illogical; or crazy. Our fears can make us do all sorts of unimaginable things, even go along with something insane as drinking cyanide laced Kool-Aid for a mass murder suicide, as was done at the urging of cult leader, Jim Jones, who "preached unconventional socialist and progressive ideas." More than 900 people, including children, who followed cult leader Jones, believed everything he told them, culminating in taking their own lives.

For anyone who's heard this story, they thought Jones, and all the people who followed him were completely crazy. It's interesting to know that at the height of its popularity during the 1970's, Jim Jones' congregation, called the "People's Temple", had a membership estimated in the thousands, and was courted by local politicians in San

Francisco, including Harvey Milk. People don't join cults because they believe its leader is crazy. They join them because they trust and believe in its leader, and "even decades later, survivors of Jonestown still remember being part of a church/organization that they devoted a good portion of their lives to, and remember the people of the organization being incredible people who were capable of committing themselves to something outside of their own self-interests" (Chiu 2020).

The popular expression, "drinking the Kool-Aid" comes from the Jonestown massacre, so when we hear it being said today, we don't necessarily think of people drinking cyanide laced Kool-Aid. We think of it more in terms of going along with the program, whatever that program is, and if someone drank the Kool-Aid, that means they've been convinced, or even brainwashed to do it. I heard the expression, "drank the Kool-Aid", more times than I can remember, during the pandemic. Because the pandemic was based on tremendous fear that we could die because of a novel virus that "allegedly" came from a bat — the moment it appeared throughout the entire world, like a global tsunami, everyone was on high alert that death was imminent, and no one was safe from contracting Covid-19 unless they adhered to, or went along with exactly what we were being told to do. As if in unison, like a finely tuned, brilliantly orchestrated, pre-meditatively prepared pandemic protocol, everyone, in every country went into lockdown (except the ones that thought for themselves like Sweden). In the article "No Lockdowns, No Mask Mandate: Sweden as a Case Study in What to Do (and Not Do) during a Pandemic 2021", Sweden's death rate is lower than other European countries that locked down and required masks, like France, Italy, and Spain. Practically everyone in the world went into lockdown, and immediate interventions and measures like "social-distancing" were put into place to stop the spread of this highly contagious disease that could kill you if you didn't maintain a physical distance between yourself and other people, which included loved ones.

Suddenly, everyone was in an unnatural state of fight or flight, and if someone came within less than 6 feet away from you, it was hard not to think, they could be your killer. I still remember vividly, when we were "allowed" to go to the market, and the fear in people's eyes if you came anywhere near them while quickly grabbing toilet paper (if you could find it), you would push your cart as fast as you could to get away from them. People were terrified. And, if you coupled that with your own personal fears, it was very easy, out of desperation, to do whatever you could to keep yourself safe and alive, even if that meant to rat out your neighbor, if they weren't complying with social distancing or wearing a mask.

The exaggerated behaviors we saw, especially by people who were in a noticeable fear state that they could die, were so afraid, you could immediately sense it, and feel it in their energy (those are also the ones that probably wear a mask in the car when they're alone). And it was those people who were also visibly angry at others who weren't quick to go along with the program that was being mandated by our government and health officials, but instead needed more time to figure out how to be with this alleged global death threat in a way that felt right, or made sense to them. There were times that I felt I was living amongst people who would stop at nothing to protect themselves from danger, and that meant going after someone verbally with hostility, because they were not doing exactly as they were, or believing every single thing that Anthony Fauci was pontificating. They (which could have been you), were perceived as the enemy, whether they had the virus, or not. It's as if you were refusing to play "Simon Says", and that infuriated those that felt you needed to go along with absolutely everything that was being told to us, which makes me wonder if that could have meant even drinking cyanide laced Kool-Aid, if they absolutely felt was necessary to avoid suffering a tortuous death with Covid-19. I had Covid, and yes it was very unpleasant. It felt like a bad flu, unlike one I've had before. I had Delta, the worst of the strains, and the best way I can describe it is it felt as if I was attacked by a bioweapon, which according to the Journal of Clinical Studies & Medical Case Reports, I probably was. (Skopec 2020). The human body is so intelligent. It knows what it knows, and does all it can to protect us and heal, which is why we should never make light of, or discount natural immunity. I survived Covid, yet the level of fear many people felt over catching it (which was constantly being driven into us on the news), made it out to be like it was the most God-awful thing you could get, and was going to ravage you like some kind of flesh-eating disease. Please know that I am not making light of the seriousness of the Covid-19 virus, and acknowledge that many people got seriously ill from it, and even died. But, through my endless amount of research because I wanted to know more than what we were being told, I also came to know from the doctors I listened to, who again, were highly professional and credible (but we were only allowed to listen to Dr. Fauci the entire time, which makes no sense, whatsoever), that many people who did die from the virus had underlying health conditions, and some were obese, or had co-morbidity, which I don't recall ever being mentioned on the news.

Look, I don't really believe that those people who were terrified, would have drank cyanide laced Kool-Aid to escape catching something that scared the living daylights out of them, and know it sounds extreme. But what leads up to an insane act like that is trusting someone to protect you from harms' way, only realizing when it's too late, that they were ill-equipped to protect you all along, and it was you that needed to decide how to best stay alive, not out of desperation, but out of common sense, and healthy discernment, which you have, if you are awake. People who are truly awake, do not follow other people who lead them to places that could harm them, and sense before it happens that they are not to be trusted. And, having healthy discernment means that you have the ability to judge well; that which seems reasonable to you, and that which does not. There were so many things we were told were going to happen during the pandemic, and because we were in a state of emergency, rolling out a Covid-19 vaccine under the name "operation warp speed", was promised to be the very thing that would save us from dying. Going along with something with such a horrible name as "operation warp speed", and not questioning it, makes me wonder how quickly we can drink the (mind-programming) "Kool-Aid", when we are told to.

People who are awake have a very good inner barometer that tells them immediately when something isn't right. What about "operation warp speed" feels right to you? And, what about a vaccine that was produced during "operation warp speed", and never went through proper clinical trials, feels right to you? And, what about not knowing what is in the Covid-19 vaccines that were quickly rolled out during "operation warp speed", especially Pfizer, which you won't know entirely what's in it for another 55 years, feels right to you? What doesn't feel right to me, is what doesn't feel right to me, and I don't need to qualify that to anyone. If I can't trust my own intuition, or my inner guidance to tell me what feels right, then I will need someone else to tell me what does, and that is where craziness begins. It starts with needing to be told what to think, or do, and not trusting yourself enough to know that if "it looks like a duck, swims like a duck, and quacks like a duck, it probably is a duck." If you see a duck, and insist it is something else, I'm afraid you might be suffering from "doublethink", which comes from George Orwell's omniscient book, *1984*. "Doublethink" is "the act of simultaneously accepting two mutually con-tradictory beliefs as true" ("Big Brother and Other Terms from '1984'" 2019).

Slogans like, "war is peace", "freedom is slavery", "ig-norance is strength", and one that we have heard recently, which should indicate that things have gone awry, "2 + 2 = 5", are examples of using "logic against logic", or sus-pending your disbelief in the contradiction. In Orwell's book *1984*, Doublethink is used as a process of indoctri-nation. The main character, Winston, has to use it in order to "accept his torturers words as true." As his memory was being erased, Doublethink was the way to be compliant and obedient to stay alive in a totalitarian state. This is what I said earlier. If your need to survive supersedes a need to know the truth, even if it is hard to accept or bare, then you will turn a duck into whatever you have to, if it means believing it will keep you on track to survive.

"Doublethink" is another thing that has become our "new normal." Men are now called women, biology doesn't matter, pedophilia has been redefined, having sex at 12 is "sexual expression", gender pronouns are taking the place of someone's name, and breastfeeding is now called "chestfeeding" (Shriver, 2021). And this is being dictated by those who "preach unconventional socialist and progressive ideas." Isn't that what they said Jim Jones did? The world does seem like it's upside down, and more and more people are using "logic against logic", which is frightening, but craziness didn't just start with the pandemic. The pandemic is what exposed the craziness that has been there all along, we just didn't want to see it, which is what deliberate unconsciousness is, that I spoke about earlier. It's convenient to turn away, or stay ignorant when we don't want to know or accept things that are uncomfortable for us, or disrupt our world in ways we cannot tolerate. But unfortunately things will only get even more crazy, if we do not wake up, and see things for what they truly are, as hard as that may be for those who refuse to awaken.

It is a universal necessity for the protection of our humanity, at this point, and Frank Herbert says it well:

"Without change, something sleeps inside us, and seldom awakens. The sleeper must awaken."

CHAPTER 8

Mindfulness and Awakening

Mindfulness means being awake.
It means knowing what you're doing.

- JON KABAT ZINN

Becoming awake involves seeing our confusion
more clearly.

- RUMI

Unless we make a concerted effort to be fully present in a moment, we cannot be aware of all of the layers, nuances, truths, or lies, that a single moment contains. That is why practicing Mindfulness helps us be present in the moment with total awareness so that we miss nothing. At a time when we are busier, more rushed, more distracted, and bombarded with so much information, it's easy to tune out as a way to shield or protect ourselves from over-stimulation and feeling overwhelmed with everything that is coming at us constantly. And there was so much coming at us over the last few years during the pandemic, one of the coping mechanisms was to tune out, or shut down; even anesthetize ourselves from feeling anxious about everything that we were needing to think about, or process daily.

As I mentioned earlier, more people turned to drugs, alcohol, even suicide during the pandemic, to stop the incessant negative news, social-media mania, and all the emotional discomfort they were feeling. The pandemic single-handedly destroyed more people's lives, even killing them, and a high percentage of that was people who didn't even get Covid. As I mentioned earlier, the closing of businesses, loss of jobs, family feuding, break-ups, and divorces; caused more people to feel disheartened, despondent, and even completely hopeless.

So, what could have helped them, and continue to help us when everything just feels as if it's getting harder, and more difficult to navigate in our lives? Mindfulness, which is focusing your awareness on the present moment, and being with what you're feeling as an observer, rather than a reactor (as you do in a formal practice of sitting meditation), is an extremely helpful tool we can use to not be at the effect of everything that is assaulting our senses daily. It is an inherent quality that each of us has, but don't always use, and if we remind ourselves to use it, it can be extremely beneficial in getting us through the difficult moments of our life. I call it a "superpower", and believe it is the number one thing that addresses non-awareness or ignorance, at its most fundamental level. When you make a conscious effort to be more present in the moments of your life, it starts to heighten your awareness in such a way that you feel as if you can see and intuit things more sharply. The layers, nuances, truths, or lies, I mentioned, are noticed very quickly, as if you have a laser sharp ability to catch everything that is happening in front of you, and in your environment. Rather than succumbing to something like fear, which gripped an entire world because of a virus, and put people in a highly unnatural state of fight or flight, which lasted the entire time of the pandemic, and still has people in fear (imagine how stressful that is to the nervous system), Mindfulness calms the mind to cultivate clarity of thought, which immediately brings down levels of Cortisol, the steroid hormone our adrenal gland produces when we're in a fight or flight response. Again, think of how extremely unnatural it is to be in an alarmed, fearful state for an extended period of

time. And, if we're always going to be at the effect of our
health organizations declaring a "state of emergency" over
a new virus or feel the threat of being put in lockdown
again, our adrenals will be completely blown out, and our
stress levels will be off the charts.

Mindfulness helps you to not readily succumb to believing that your survival is being threatened just because
you are told that it is. This very intelligent practice helps
you take a mindful pause to check in with your feelings
and emotions, so that you can make a measured decision
for yourself, based on what your own logic, and reasoning
ability is telling you, because you gave yourself the time to
think things through carefully, rather than to act quickly,
or impulsively, which we tend to do when we are overtak-
en by our emotions, especially fear. When we do something as simple as take a deep breath before we react, and
identify exactly what is going on, we won't be so quick
to take the next step forward, unless we feel that we are
doing it from a place of mental clarity, and equanimity.

Keep in mind that if you are constantly told to be
afraid, you can go into a hypnotic state without even
realizing it. Repeating words and phrases like, the "new
normal", or the "war against the unvaccinated", can have
a hypnotic power, and for someone who doesn't practice Mindfulness, or take that necessary pause before
reacting to something, they can be more influenced by
power words and phrases, especially if they are repeated

by others who they view as an expert, or hold a position of authority. Mindfulness not only helps you take that mindful pause to not quickly react to your feelings and emotions that might be triggered by outside influences, but it also helps you be fully present in a moment so you can ask yourself questions with cognitive awareness, like, "why am I feeling what I am?" or "who is telling me to feel this way?" or "why do I believe I have to think and feel what I do?", or "do I have power over how I think or feel?", and most importantly, "am I letting others determine how I feel, or influence my decisions?" This pause is essential, and necessary, especially when we are in the midst of a situation that feels alarming, or we are told we should feel frightened because whatever that situation is, it's completely out of our control, but don't have enough information to verify if that is true, and decide how we should best handle it.

Mindfulness also helps you exercise critical thinking, which is almost impossible to do when you're in a fight or flight response. It helps us mindfully decide that we don't need to accept fear just because we are told that we should be fearful, and consciously release fear-based thoughts from our mind and body before it turns into anxiety or depression, which can cause illness. The pandemic caused more people to go into a complete state of fearful reactivity, and studies found that, "anti-anxiety medication prescription spiked 34% during the pandemic" (Wehrwein

67

2011). However, if people were more versed in Mindfulness, which helps you stay in a state of mental calmness, I believe they would have made very different decisions for themselves that would have served their wellbeing for the better. One should never make major decisions, especially when it comes to your health, when you are in a mental state of fear, and we were provoked to be in a state of fear constantly, which felt inescapable. When you diligently practice Mindfulness, you do not give into emotional ups and downs, but instead, are fully aware of what is causing those emotional upheavals, and work with them with a keen understanding of how to move through the energy with grace, and keep your mind open. That is when you can think clearly, and manage your thoughts and feelings to know, again, why you are experiencing them. It's very important to ask ourselves what is causing our fear. Is it because of what we are hearing and being told, or is it coming from our own mind, where we have carefully formulated our own thoughts, ideas, and conclusions.

Mindfulness will help you become a very sharp thinker and be more discerning of thoughts that are your own, or thoughts that are being influenced by others.

CHAPTER 9

The Power
Of Metacognition

Think of Mindfulness as an innate superpower. It's like having metacognition, which means you have a heightened awareness of what you're thinking in the moment, as well as a heightened awareness of your understanding of what you're thinking, and why.

- ORA NADRICH

Mindfulness and Mysticism: Connecting Present Moment Awareness with Higher States of Consciousness

I want to bring up this movement of transhumanism, again. I find it interesting that we feel we need to "enhance the human organism with the fundamental aim to modify it so radically as to overcome fundamental human limitations", but we don't even consider what the human organism is capable of, in its natural brilliance. This aim, or "goal" of transhumanism is fraught with so many disturbing things, I fear it will completely discard any human potential, or abilities that we naturally have to transcend our human limitations with something like Mindfulness. When we naturally heighten our awareness, we are able to utilize aspects of ourselves that are quite powerful, so why don't we trust Mindfulness enough to develop it more (even teach it to children in schools to help with emotional intelligence, which I will speak about more later), and use it as a true superpower?

"Meta", in colloquial English, means "extremely self-aware, self-reflective, or self-referential." It comes from the Greek prefix and proposition, meta, which means "after" or "beyond" and when combined with words in English, meta means "change" or "alteration". Mindfulness creates something called "metacognition", which is a heightened awareness and understanding of one's own thought process. It's very important to be aware of our thoughts, so that we can work with them in a way that helps with things like negative thought patterns, which can create conditions like anxiety and depression. When "meta" is used with something like Meta-verse, it clearly means changing and altering the universe, so if you're having a more heightened awareness of changing or altering the universe, it's important to be that much more aware, as to how. Are we altering the universe by creating a digital version of it, where you spend your time immersed in a virtual reality, and connect with other 3D people (avatars)? People might say, well, that's "another" universe, not the "actual" one. I understand that, but if you present a virtual universe to escape into, especially for adolescents, whose psyches and prefrontal cortexes are still developing, aren't you running the risk of increasing things like mental disorders, anxiety, or even addiction? This "other" universe doesn't seem to be doing a better job of addressing problems like mental disorders, and could in fact, be creating more of it than the "real" universe does. According to an article on the Negative Effects of Gaming, "in 2020 there were an estimated 2.7 billion gamers worldwide, and the number is still rising" (Adair 2021).

And here's the sad truth, unfortunately more people will know what the Metaverse is, and less about metacognition. We live in a time where valuing things like being a more aware, conscious human being who's in touch with their thoughts and feelings, just can't compete with billion-dollar businesses like video games, and a new super-hyped virtual universe, estimated to become an $800 billion-dollar market by 2024 (Joshi 2022).

Who needs to be mindful, or extremely self-aware, self-reflective, or self-referential, when you don't have to be aware of anything other than escaping into a virtual reality where you can be completely free of any mental disorders, even though being there might cause you to get one. The article says that "many experts look at the metaverse as a 3D model of the internet. Basically, a place parallel to the physical world, where you spend your digital life." And, as we know, people are spending more time in their "digital life" than they prefer spending in a non-digital one, which is why the Metaverse seems so concerning, again, especially for young people. The article goes on to ask, "but what even is this metaverse? Is it a virtual universe with endless possibilities we can escape into? Is it the dystopian future of the internet built on speculative sci-fi?" (Joshi 2022).

I think asking, "is it the dystopian future of the internet" an extremely important question. We must ask ourselves what is really going on during this extremely fast changing time we are living in, and be very mindfully aware of what it is. Dystopian fiction is very hot right now, and sales of George Orwell's *1984*, Margaret Atwood's *The Handmaid's Tale*, and movies like *Outbreak* and *12 Monkeys* have skyrocketed since 2016. Could it be that people are relating to dystopian themes, and according to an article in The Conversation "Are we living in dystopia?", people might be feeling that they are. The article presents some very thought-provoking ideas, like, "Dystopia is not a real place, it is a warning, usually about something bad the government is doing or something good it is failing to do. Actual dystopias are fictional, but real-life governments can be dystopian – as in, looking a lot like fiction" (Atchison and Shames 2020).

So, here we are dealing with things in "real-life", like failing governments, and escaping into a virtual reality (Metaverse), where according to technologists, "the metaverse will take the virtual reality experience to the next level, allowing users to float into the virtual world to do everything from buy land and host parties to even get married through digital avatars" (Joshi 2022). That sounds like escapism to a tee, especially since it excludes the real-life dystopian problems we are witnessing in our actual universe. Having a mindful awareness of this is extremely important, because once we don't acknowledge and address our real-life problems, and instead choose to escape from them, our world will look "a lot like fiction", which it already does. And, if we lose sight of reality, our senses will become so dull, or numbed out, we will no longer be able to properly identify genuine problems, like a failing government, for what it truly is. This is what makes me want to literally shake people and say, "wake up!" Or would you prefer the quote I shared earlier – "The universe has shaken you to awaken you". How the universe could shake you, might not be as gently as I would. The universe gives us all sorts of messages constantly, for us to awaken, but most people don't see them, or want to.

I have no doubt there is so much going on today that feels as if we are living in dystopian times, that a lot of people just can't handle or accept it. That, unfortunately, will do us no good at all, and I can only hope and pray that more people will awaken to recognize that we must acknowledge the problems we are facing, so that we can do something about them, immediately. In the article "Are we living in dystopia?" it says, "dystopia is a warning about how bad the government is doing, or something good it is failing to do" (Atchison and Shames 2020), and I happen to agree with that. We must speak of these things without allowing for the weaponization of politics. During the last few years, it was almost impossible to speak about the problems we were having without it turning into political weaponry, which felt divisive, and fueled polarization between us. It seems, there is such a level of denial about the problems we are facing, that I feel there are people who would rather protect a failing government and a lack of good, reliable leadership, than admit to the problems that are so blatantly obvious.

When you practice Mindfulness, you see things as they really are, and don't make excuses for it. And, if, or when, you want to escape the unpleasant truths, you are fully aware of your need to escape, which will make it harder for you to do. Mindfulness keeps you in the present moment, as uncomfortable as it may be, and helps you work through it with total awareness. It makes us stronger, and more conscious human beings, so that we can accept what the present moment is showing us, and work with it to problem solve, intelligently, both for ourselves, and others. Mindfulness also helps us be more benevolent, and compassionate people, something I think is lacking in some people, especially those that are trying to catapult us into what feels like a dystopian future. People like Mark Zuckerberg, Bill Gates, Klaus Schwab, and others, who feel they must monopolize our lives by telling us how to live because they are wealthy, and amongst the global elites. They do not seem like mindful, consciously aware people. And the future that I envision for the human race is very different than the one they seem to want for us, which feels very devoid of Mindfulness.

When you are truly present, and consciously aware, you do not have a need to escape the moments of your life, but instead, feel grateful to be alive in each, and every moment you are in. I hope that more people will not have a need to escape this reality by choosing things like substances, or a virtual world, but instead, have the courage to face the problems and obstacles we are encountering, and know that they have the natural superpower with Mindfulness and metacognition, to rise above it.

The Signs Of Awakening

The solution to the problem of the day is
the awakening of the consciousness of humanity
to the divinity within.

- HAZRAT INAYAT KHAN

Times are difficult globally; awakening is no
longer a luxury or an ideal. It's becoming critical.
We don't need to add more depression, more
discouragement, or more anger to what's already
here. It's becoming essential that we learn how to
relate sanely with difficult times. The earth seems to
be beseeching us to connect with joy and discover
our innermost essence. This is the best way that we
can benefit others.

- PEMA CHODRON

A spiritual awakening is the most profound shift of consciousness that a human being can experience. When it happens, it's as if you suddenly have a profound understanding of why you incarnated into this lifetime, and what it is you are meant to do here on planet earth. You feel ready to know the truths of the universe, and all that is false, falls away.

There are people who want to realize this shift of consciousness, and feel the only way they can, is to take psychedelics, or plant medicine (like Ayahuasca), which has become popular, and I believe the reason for that is more people want to awaken. But that isn't the only way to awaken, although there are those who feel they've had a shift in consciousness on psychedelics, or plant medicine. That is not the path I encourage to take for a spiritual awakening because I feel that one can attain it on their own, naturally, but I will leave that up to you, as to how you think you can open yourself up to awakening, if you are truly ready to.

So, how does one know they are ready for a spiritual awakening? The best way I can answer that is, you will know. And it will not be your ego telling you. As a matter of fact, a spiritual awakening makes you confront your ego in such a way that you awaken up out of identification with the ego, and realize your true self other than the false self, which you have believed yourself to be. Our false self is who we think we are as our main identity, rather than our true, soul essence, which is who we came into the world as, and who we know we must return to. A spiritual awakening is like coming home to the authentic self, and for those who experience it, they feel as if they are reborn to who they really are, and everything they've gone through has helped prepare them for their awakening.

There are people who have always sensed that there is something more in this life to know and don't go along with the program, or any program, for that matter, that leads them away from discovering the truths of the universe, and why we are here. Suffice it to say, there are those who lead themselves, and are more likely to seek out a spiritual awakening that will reveal the truths of the universe to them, and others that are more inclined to be led, and follow a path that most people, or the masses, are on. If you are someone who does not wish to know the truth beyond the systems that govern us, then you are not likely to go beyond being governed and are satisfied with how you are guided and instructed to live on the life journey. Those people that adhere to governance and don't question it, are the ones that are quick to defend whatever is governing them, even if it is misleading. The reason for that is they are not ready to step out of the Matrix, and by that, I mean, reality as you have believed it to be, which hides the truth from humanity, so that you can be dependent on those in power to control you.

If at this point in the book, you are still thinking that

this is based on conspiracy theories, or don't understand why I'm using a fictional movie, *The Matrix*, as an example of hidden truths, then maybe you should put it down and stop reading it. We are doing our humanity a terrible disservice by not speaking out about these things, which might seem too unconventional to grasp. Quickly labeling everything that goes beyond a type of thinking that is based on conventionality, at the expense of individuality, is extremely limited. And I believe, this labeling happens because some people feel safer with a type of thinking that doesn't question things on a much deeper level, because, as I mentioned earlier, they just don't want to disrupt their world in any way, especially if it means acknowledging the possibility that they are being deceived and lied to by the very people who tell them what to do, or how to live.

But, if you are thinking, "yes, I am ready to awaken", which I hope that you are, let's continue on with some signs of awakening, so that you can prepare yourself for what's coming, which will require you to be as awake as you possibly can. There is a new world upon us, and I can assure you that it is not a "New World Order", which someone like Klaus Schwab, the founder of the World Economic Forum, wants us to believe that it is. He feels that in their world, you will "own nothing, have no privacy, and life will never be better" (Auken 2016).

An awakened person knows they have rights and

choices, and uses them to imagine a life they have chosen for themselves, because they imagine a life that they,
and only them, envisions. This New World Order simply
means nothing other than world governance, as opposed
to individual sovereignty and self-governance, and again,
if you're someone who wants to be governed, then you
will find no reason to question this tyrannical agenda that
is being set into motion by global elites, of which you and
I are not one of.

As I said, the most powerful path to be on is one of
knowledge and information, which leads to wisdom and
freedom. So, let's discuss what you are going to experience
as you embark on this monumental path of awakening
that will give you the greatest knowledge, wisdom, and
freedom, you can have.

Here are some signs that you are on the path of a
spiritual awakening:

1. You sense that something life-changing is
   happening to you.

2. Your intuition is laser sharp.

3. You can sense dishonesty, deception, manipulation,
   and inauthenticity, immediately, which makes it
   hard or impossible for you to be fooled, coerced,

lied to or controlled. It's as if your truth barometer is turned up way high.

4. You feel more connected to spirituality. It might be a connection to God, or a divine source you feel you are in alignment with.

5. You are able to let go of attachment to material things, which no longer defines you or your self-worth.

6. You can immediately sense like-minded people. Those that are awake are recognizing one another quickly.

7. Your relationships are shifting, and you no longer want to be around people that aren't on the same vibrational frequency as you. Those that are like-minded can feel like your tribe or spiritual family.

8. You are getting mental downloads of important information you feel ready to receive.

9. You are experiencing things like Déjà vu (a feeling of having already experienced something, or knowing that what you are experiencing was meant to be); seeing synchronicities (coincidental occurrence of events), which psychologist Carl Jung felt can hold potent spiritual powers; having mystical

experiences, which can be an awareness of a divine truth you are ready to know, and perceiving it as transcendental, meaning it goes beyond the regular physical realm, making you feel connected, or "at one with" everything.

10. Your dreams are more vivid, and filled with archetypal symbolism with deep meaning. Your unconscious is giving you valuable information you need to have at this exact time.

11. You feel an inner calm of deep wisdom, as if you are fully prepared to take on the profound changes we are experiencing with this Great Awakening.

12. You do not fear death, and know that this spiritual shift is divided between those that fear death, and doing all they can to hold onto life with desperation. And those that are not ruled by fear, trust that death is part of the journey of transcendence.

13. You know with certainty that you are the one manifesting your reality and directing your destiny, and it is only you who has the power to do so.

You might be experiencing other things, indicating that you are on the path of a spiritual awakening. Whatever it is you are feeling, know that you have made the absolute right decision to be an awakened one, and the farther you go on the journey of awakening, the more you will know that you are manifesting your own reality, each step of the way. Those that think they can control our destiny, are in for a rude awakening, not a spiritual one. During this historical time of a great spiritual awakening, time will reveal who will stand mighty as divine warriors, and who will fall from a megalomaniacal delusion.

CHAPTER 11

What To Be Aware Of In Your Awakening

All truth passes through three stages.
First, it is ridiculed. Second, it is violently opposed.
Third, it is accepted as being self-evident.

- ARTHUR SCHOPENHAUER

When we are in the awakening process it does not mean that our awareness can lag in any way. As a matter of fact, the more we awaken the sharper our awareness must become. Yes, it will become sharper because awakening puts us in a natural state of heightened awareness, but the daily bombardment of over-information-stimulation, as well as, indoctrination, is a constant assault to our senses, so it's natural to want to occasionally take a break from it and mentally rest. However, like a warrior who sleeps with one eye open to keep a watch out for its enemy, and not be thrown off guard, we must think of our awareness as something that never sleeps.

Becoming an awakened warrior is not something one should take lightly. I know it may sound hyperbolic to say that we are in a spiritual war, but if you think otherwise, and want to believe it's just another day in paradise, I would cool it on the mind controlling Kool-Aid. Think of awakening as being sober to the truth, and, in-as-much as the truth can make us want to numb out, or anesthetize ourselves from it, I'm sorry to say that the only way the truth can set us free, is to remove anything that interferes with having complete soundness of mind to see the truth for what it is.

There is a tendency to avoid, deny, or even intoxicate ourselves from the truth, and I can see why they kept the liquor stores open the entire time during the lockdown, and considered it an "essential business." You know what is most essential? To be awake at a time when the powers that be want to keep you anesthetized and intoxicated as much as possible, so that you believe what you are told like a good, dutiful citizen, and question no one, especially authority. If this sounds like constant work, it is, and I know how most people dread having to work so hard to be an awake, conscious human being. Wouldn't it be great if there was a pill for waking up? Well, actually there is.

It's called the "red pill", which refers to "a choice between the willingness to learn a potentially unsettling or life-changing truth…or remaining in contented ignorance with the blue pill" ("Red Pill and Blue Pill" 2020). The terms refer to a scene in the 1999 film, *The Matrix*, and how apt it is for what's taking place right now. I know it's not pleasant to compare the times we are in to movies like *The Matrix*, books like Orwell's *1984*, and even one of the darkest, most evil times in history, Nazi Germany and World War II, but I think it's actually fortunate that we have things to compare the times we are in, so that we can know what is possible, and that there were others before us who encountered, or perceived similar insanity and atrocities as we are. And hopefully we will be quicker in responding to it than allowing for another type of Holocaust.

As you awaken more, life will throw you curve balls along the way, to test and see how awake you really are, and if you're being vigilant about staying awake. You will be judged, ridiculed, challenged, even hated by others (sadly, even members of your own family), who are annoyed and agitated at your almost incessant need to question the narratives that are being imposed on us daily, by people in positions of power and authority — like our government, and health officials. You will find that those people who are hell-bent on believing literally everything that is being told to them by anyone who they perceive is in a position of authority, will look at you with fire in their eyes, and have been known to raise their voices almost immediately when you question what they believe in. Many people who have experienced this, say it feels as if they want to undermine your opinion, and insultingly, question your intelligence, even if you're a Ph.D., or have a law-degree. It's mind-boggling how people in their own esteemed professions are calling them out as a conspiracy theorist, if they speak out against the Covid-19 narrative, which has become the rote response from their opposers. What happened to civil discourse, which is intended to enhance understanding?

Something seems to happen to them, as if a knee-jerk reaction, when you question the narrative that has been shoved down our throats for two years. And why is it so hard for them to accept that maybe you don't believe, or want to go along with what the officials, or alleged experts say, that they trust 100%, and even willingly gave their body over to inject with a genetic experiment. Have you noticed, or encountered someone who immediately gets pissed off for even suggesting they could be wrong? And if you say things like, "I don't trust the Covid-19 shot", or "there were things about the pandemic that just didn't make sense" or "the media is biased", or the worst offense, "we are being lied to," they can look as if they want to kill you. In their mind, you are the one who could kill them, by not going along with the fear mongering narrative we were being fed the entire pandemic, to "supposedly" stay alive, and still being fed fear by hearing the government, and health officials say that we're still in a state of emergency, which we know is a lie. Are they going to drag this state of emergency out forever, even after the CDC came out and changed their guidelines, no longer requiring quarantining, and confirmed that neither the vaccine, or the masks prevent getting Covid-19, or transmitting it? Dr. Rochelle Walensky, the director of the Centers for Disease Control and Prevention, "delivered a sweeping rebuke of her agency's handling of the coronavirus pandemic", and said that "to be frank, we are responsible for some pretty dramatic, pretty public mistakes" (LaFraniere 2022). And yet, even after these health officials are changing their tune we're still in a state of emergency? Please pay attention to what is logical, and what is not. And, if what you say elicits a defensive, or harsh response in anyone who has bought the narrative (or drank the Kool-Aid), know that the reason for that is, you are threatening their sense of reality, and that is off limits to them. But, maybe you should ask them if it's off limits to question the authorities who keep moving the goal post every time we are being told to get one more Covid-19 experimental shot (how many will ever be enough), or comply to one more unnatural physical thing to keep ahead of a novel virus, that maybe we just need to accept living with?

They might vehemently dislike you questioning

authority, and even want to punish you for it, but you might agree with this quote by Albert Einstein, "To punish me for my contempt for authority, fate made me an authority myself." Become an authority of the very things you believe in, so that you can back up what you're saying with factual information and knowledge, which you have worked so hard to obtain. One of the things I will say about people who have been unfairly accused of being conspiracy theorists during this censorship and cancel-culture era, like Robert F. Kennedy, Jr., is that they worked tirelessly to research the very things they knew must be questioned. Robert's book, *The Real Anthony Fauci*, was highly recommended on Joe Rogan's podcast to the chagrin of the "misinformation police". They were equally annoyed when Dr. Robert Malone was on Rogan's show, and he's the inventor of the mRNA technology. There were others, like Robert F. Kennedy, Jr., who became their own authority because they genuinely wanted to help people by giving them, not "misinformation", but more (even scientific) information so they could decide what is best for them. As I mentioned, Dr. Vladimir Zelenko, strongly believed in the Ivermectin therapeutic protocol he used to help his patients recover from Covid before it was falsely labeled as a "horse de-wormer" (and clearly not profitable for big pharma). He was so committed to helping people, and keeping them informed about medical truth, as doctors are meant to do. Sadly, he passed away from cancer. He, like Robert F. Kennedy, Jr., was a fearless warrior, fighting for people's freedom. Watch, if it is still up, his last health update from the hospital before he died – Facebook ("Dr. Vladimir Zev Zelenko" 2022). These honorable men, (and there are many of them, some who I have mentioned in this book), have said that they are prepared to "die on this hill" for the truth to be known. That's how important it is for them to tell the world what they feel is so urgent for us to know. I would take anyone who is willing to die for the truth, very, very seriously. This war against the freedom of our humanity is the hill you'd want to die on, if that meant you would have to succumb to tyranny to stay alive.

What is the most important thing for you to be aware of in your awakening? To know that you are willing to fight for (maybe even die), for your loved ones, and for our entire humanity so the truth can be known.

CHAPTER 12

Stages Of Spiritual Growth

Life is growth. If we stop growing, technically and
spiritually, we are as good as dead.

- MORIHEI UESHIBA

The path of spiritual growth is a path of lifelong
learning.

- M. SCOTT PECK

For those who value growing spiritually, they know it is
a "path of lifelong learning", as M. Scott Peck says, and
that it takes commitment and patience to evolve. We don't
embark on a spiritual path to hurry the process along, but
instead cherish the learning, which means each stage of it.

As Ralph Waldo Emerson said, "It's not the destination, it's the journey", and for those who understand that, they know that each stage of the spiritual journey, is a very important one, and no matter where you are on it, you will learn exactly what you need for your spiritual growth.

I'd like to use the Noble Eightfold Path of Buddha's teachings as a guideline for the stages of spiritual growth. It was intended to be the path to end ignorance and suffering, which I believe is what is afflicting our world today, and lead us to enlightenment by cultivating wisdom and compassion. We seem to be stuck in a type of mass unconsciousness that is getting in the way of our spiritual growth, individually and collectively, and something like following the Eightfold Path can teach us how to become wiser, more compassionate beings, which we can be, if we choose to awaken.

The Eightfold Path consists of:

1. Right View

2. Right Thought

3. Right Speech

4. Right Action

5. Right Livelihood

6. Right Effort

7. Right Mindfulness

8. Right Concentration

Here are each Noble Truth, and how it applies to the times we are in presently:

1. Right View – This Noble Truth is a significant first step on the path, as it relates to seeing the world and everything in it, as it really is, not as we believe, or want it to be. For the last few years, our perceptions of how we saw the world, and everything that was going on with the pandemic, seemed so diametric; we were divided into two groups of people who felt that their view was the right one. Right View cannot be realized until we see the world and everything in it as it truly is, as difficult as that may be, especially when we want it to be different than what it actually is. If there is a distortion in perception out of fear, which has been the dominate state of mind that millions of people have had during the pandemic, Right View cannot be realized. The only way for Right View to be realized collectively, is when all beings awaken from the slumber of illusion.

2. Right Thought - According to Buddha, our thoughts are very powerful. He said, "The mind is everything. What we think, we become." If we hold thoughts of love and non-violence, and extend it to all beings, this is what we will manifest in the world. And, if we hold thoughts of selfish desire, ill-will, hatred and violence, that is what we will manifest in the world. Each of us can hold thoughts of love and non-violence, and in our meditation and prayers, can extend it to all sentient beings that we share this earth with. At this time of polarization, confusion, and dissent, we must ask ourselves, "Am I holding Right Thoughts in my mind, and what are my intentions with these thoughts?"

3. Right Speech – This is the ability to speak, the intelligence to speak (the thought behind speech) and the speaking itself. What I will add to this is freedom of speech, which means "the right to express any opinions without censorship or restraint", and that right has been violated during this time of cancel-culture. I'm not condoning speech that is not of Right Thought, and filled with ill-will, hatred and violence, but if we do not allow for the speaking itself, and try to control others because we don't agree with the thoughts behind their speech, we are disregarding the Noble Truth of Right Speech. I don't believe Buddha felt that a select group of people in power should be the arbiters of what constitutes Right Speech, according to their orders they feel others must obey, but,

rather, it is incumbent upon each of us to be fully aware and mindful of the thoughts we are choosing to speak, and use our intelligence to speak before we do. Keep in mind, that if one cannot say something useful, one should keep noble silence.

4. Right Action – This aims at promoting moral, honorable, and peaceful conduct, which has been disrupted by our polarization and dissent during these challenging times. With millions of people feeling fearful about their health, well-being, and experiencing tremendous financial losses due to businesses closing because of the pandemic, it has not engendered moral, honorable, and peaceful conduct. Instead, it has provoked immoral and dishonorable behaviors, as well as increased acts of violence. Right Action admonishes that we should abstain from destroying life, from stealing, and dishonest dealings, and yet, with more people feeling hopeless and desperate, rioting and looting has increased, destroying many businesses, and the communities they are in. With Right Action, we act rightly, and wish no harm on one another, and our right actions spring from compassion, as well as, our understanding that our actions create consequences. There is a word in Buddhism, "sila", which means "morality, virtue, and ethical conduct". It points to the concept of morality as living harmoniously with others. We must come together at this time, and not allow for our moral, honorable, and peaceful conduct to be disrupted by what

we perceive and believe is threatening us because we are told that we are not healthy, capable, and strong. Instead, let us choose Right Thought, Right Speech, and Right Action to unite us, and bring the world together for the New World that we are imagining in our collective vision.

5. Right Livelihood – This means that each of us has a right to engage in an occupation that not only earns us a living, but also creates greater happiness, wisdom, and well-being, as well as, relieves suffering in ourselves, and others. With the Noble Truths, Right View, and Right Thought, we begin to take responsibility for our perceptions of how we see the world, and acknowledge that our thoughts are playing a significant role in how we are creating our reality. We no longer wait for others to determine our happiness and well-being, but instead know that it is our sovereign right to create the livelihood we deserve. It's important to ask ourselves how our work affects our mind and heart, and whether it is causing more value to our life, or less? What we do, and how we do it can make important contributions to others, and their well-being, and it can also do them harm. Working for companies or corporations that do not serve the well-being, health, or safety of others, and have intentions that are dubious, you might want to reconsider working in those types of unwholesome, greedy environments. Right Livelihood means that we are choosing, and performing our work, consciously, and needn't choose work

that we don't feel we can do truthfully and honorably, as the Noble Truth, Right Action, encourages us to do. This is a time when many people are re-evaluating their livelihood and making changes in their lives because they no longer want to live dishonestly, or inauthentically to who they really are. The pandemic caused a lot of people to get connected to something that feels more spiritual for them, and want to do work that aligns with their purpose and intentions. One shouldn't choose their livelihood out of fear, or because they feel they have to, but instead, pick work or a profession because you feel that you can contribute the best of your abilities and attributes. We spend so much of our lives at work, that the choice of the wrong occupation can be a major impediment to our spiritual growth. Right Livelihood supports our spiritual growth, rather than impede it.

6. Right Effort – This is the energetic will to prevent evil, and unwholesome states of mind from arising, which the Noble Truth, Right Thought, also helps us with. In order to get rid of evil, and unwholesome states that have already arisen, especially at a time when fear is dominating people's minds, causing them not to live morally, honorably, and peacefully, as the Noble Truth, Right Action, teaches us to do. We must make an effort to develop wholesome qualities in our character, and release unwholesome qualities, like greed, anger, and ignorance, which do not serve our well-being, and others. When

we cultivate wholesome qualities, like generosity, loving-kindness, and wisdom, we raise our energetic will, and help shift the energetic will of others. As Buddha said, "Set your heart on doing good. Do it over and over again, and you will be filled with joy."

7. Right Mindfulness - This is to be diligently aware, and attentive of our thoughts, feelings, and actions, so that we can practice Right Mindfulness in all that we do. Mindfulness, as I've spoken about, strengthens present moment awareness, and when we are present in the moments of our life with total awareness, we can practice the Eightfold Noble Truths, effectively. Unless one is mindful, there cannot be a Right View, thought and intention, speech, action, livelihood, effort, or concentration. Right Mindfulness is the development of an accurate and precise awareness of the present moment uncolored by ideas, or beliefs. And, at a time when we are allowing our different, or opposing ideas, and beliefs to make us less mindful of others, that is when we must be diligently aware, and practice Right Mindfulness in all of our waking moments, and with whomever we interact with. Right Mindfulness is the basis for spiritual growth, and keeps us on the right path that culminates in obtaining the knowledge, and wisdom that is needed to awaken.

8. Right Concentration – This is the final Noble Truth on the spiritual path of awakening. Practicing Right Mindfulness, we understand the importance of being in

the present moment with total awareness, but in order for us to obtain the knowledge and wisdom that is needed for awakening, we must practice Right Concentration to filter out everything except the precise knowledge that is needed, so that wisdom can be deepened, and spiritual growth can be realized. Right Concentration can be practiced in a formal sitting meditation, or contemplation, but not to the exclusion of practicing mindful awareness in all of the moments of your life. Practicing Right Concentration helps make our focus laser sharp, and as we move through each of the Noble Truths, and practice Right Concentration with each of them, we will get that much closer to the radiance of enlightenment on the life journey. Remember, it is not the destination that matters, it is the journey, so practice Right Concentration at all junctures of the journey to strengthen your spiritual growth.

What I will add to this, is to diligently stay on the path of awakening, so truths will continue to be realized. The only way for us to become aware, conscious, and ultimately, enlightened human beings, is to walk the path of awakening with a strong focus, and clear intentions. There are no short cuts on the path of awakening, and no quick remedies or fixes. Buddha didn't just become enlightened because he wanted to be. Yes, there was a deep desire in his soul, but he was a young prince who was willing to renounce all worldly things in search of the ultimate truth and enlightenment. He saw the suffering of others, and wanted to know what caused it. After wandering around for many days and nights, Gautama (Buddha, which means enlightened one) found himself near a large peepul tree, which called out to him. He made a resolution – "I shall sit under this tree and meditate upon my questions, and shall not move until I have my answers. Even if my skin rots and my body decays, I shall not budge till I see the light."

May each of us meditate upon our questions, and continue to do so, until we find the exact answers we need at this very fragile time. Let the light of truth lead us to freedom and sovereignty.

CHAPTER 13

The Great Awakening Initiation

Where there is great doubt, there will be Great Awakening, small doubt, small awakening, no doubt, no awakening.

- Zen Proverb

The conquest of fear yields the courage of life. That is the cardinal initiation of every heroic adventure – fearlessness and achievement.

- JOSEPH CAMPBELL

It is the conquest of our fear that gives us the courage to awaken, and when we overcome our fear to know the truth of this life, we will find ourselves ready to be initiated into the Great Awakening of our time. As I said earlier, you should consider yourself lucky if you are on the path of a spiritual awakening. What an incredible opportunity it is to emerge from what I called a "sleepwalker trance" and enter into a conscious state of lucid truth. For those who know this, they also know that they were born to be here at this time of the Great Awakening. If you believe that you are here for a reason, and are part of something that is beyond what you could ever have imagined, then you are ready to be initiated into the Great Awakening of our time.

Throughout history, there have been periods of Great Awakenings that refer to religious revivals when religion had grown stale, and church attendance was declining. "In the 1700's, a European movement called the Enlightenment, swept America. Also called the Age of Reason, this era laid the foundation for a scientific, rather than religious, worldview. Freedom of conscience was at the heart of this struggle against old regimes and old ways of thinking, and it changed the way people viewed authority. The Great Awakening changed the way people thought about their relationship with the divine, with themselves, and with other people. The Enlightenment engaged the mind, but the Great Awakening engaged the heart" ("The First Great Awakening: Religious Revival and American Independence - Video & Lesson Transcript," n.d.).

According to Robert William Fogel, who was awarded the Nobel Prize in Economic Science in 1993, he writes in his book, *The Fourth Great Awakening and the Future of Egalitarianism,* "to understand what is taking place today, we need to understand the nature of the recurring political-religious cycles called 'Great Awakenings.' Each lasting about 100 years, Great Awakenings consist of three phases, each about a generation long. A cycle begins with a phase of religious revival, propelled by the tendency of new technological advances to outpace the human capacity to cope with ethical and practical complexities that those new technologies entail."

So, is this where we find ourselves today? Are we facing a new Great Awakening, brought on by "the tendency of new technological advances to outpace the human capacity to cope with ethical and practical complexities that those new technologies entail?"

Some of the newest technological advancements are:

1. Artificial Intelligence (AI) – the simulation of human intelligence processed by machines, especially computer systems.

2. Virtual Reality – Computer-generated simulation of three-dimensional image of environment that can be interacted with in a seemingly real or physi-

cal way by a person using special electronic equipment.

3. Augmented Reality – A technology that superimposes a computer-generated image on a user's view of the real world.

4. 5G – The fifth generation of cellular networking. It's the next step in mobile technology, what the phones and tablets of the future will use for data, and should make our current LTE networks feel as slow and irrelevant as 3G data seems now.

5. Blockchain - A system in which a record of transaction made in bitcoin or another cryptocurrency are maintained across several computers that are linked in a peer-to-peer network.

6. Quantum Computing – A rapidly emerging technology that harnesses the laws of quantum mechanics to solve problems too complex for classical computers.

7. Cyber Security – The practice of defending computers, servers, mobile devices, electronic systems, networks, and data from malicious attacks.

We know that technology is evolving exponentially, and taking us on such a fast, accelerated journey, will it go beyond our understanding of what it means to be human, or will being human even matter, if the goal of the transhumanist movement is to become, not just transhuman, but posthuman. And, with all of these technological advancements, it's inevitable that we will try to cope with these accelerated changes, which not everyone will be able to. As I mentioned, for some people, these changes are just too overwhelming, and they are not able to cope with them in healthy ways. And for others, they will gravitate towards something like religion for answers, as many of the religious leaders of the earlier Great Awakenings, encouraged people to do. But, as I mentioned, we're living at a time when churches, temples, and mosques, are kept closed when there is something like a pandemic, and our health organizations call for a "state of emergency", citing places of worship, "non-essential businesses", which can happen again at any time.

Religion might strengthen people's faith during these challenging times, but if we allow for something like transhumanism, to take us over, where will God be found, then? In an article in the Guardian, "God in the Machine: My Strange Journey Into Transhumanism", Meghan O'Gieblyn, writes about her own religious struggles when she dropped out of Bible school and "stopped believing in God". That was when she read Ray Kurzweil's book,

The Age of Spiritual Machines, and says it was "difficult to account for the totemic power she ascribed to the book", and that she "carried it with her everywhere" (O'Gieblyn 2017). Kurzweil, Google's Director of Engineering, and a leading proponent of transhumanism philosophy, writes, "The 21st century will be different. The human species, along with the computational technology it created, will be able to solve age-old problems ... and will be in a position to change the nature of mortality in a post-biological future." O'Gieblyn explains in her article that, "like the theologians at her Bible school, Kurzweil had his own historical narrative." She writes, "he divided all of evolution into successive epochs. We were living in the fifth epoch, when human intelligence begins to merge with technology. Soon we would reach the 'Singularity', the point at which we would be transformed into what Kurzweil called 'Spiritual Machines'. We would transfer or 'resurrect' our minds onto supercomputers, allowing us to live forever. Our bodies would become incorruptible, immune to disease and decay, and we would acquire knowledge by uploading it to our brains. Nanotechnology would allow us to remake Earth into a terrestrial paradise, and then we would migrate to space, terraforming other planets. Our powers, in short, would be limitless" (O'Gieblyn 2017).

Reaching "Singularity", that Kurzweil speaks of, is a theory, which means, "superintelligence is developed and

achieved by self-directed computers." And, according to
the article "Singularity (the)" by Andrew Zola, "in technology, the singularity describes a hypothetical future
where technology growth is out of control and irrevers-
ible. These intelligent and powerful technologies will radically and unpredictably transform our reality." Zola goes
on to say that, "the singularity would involve computer
programs becoming so advanced that artificial intelligence
(AI) transcends human intelligence, potentially erasing
the boundary between humanity and computers" (I will
go into the Singularity more in depth in a later chapter).
He also mentions that "entrepreneurs and public figures
like Elon Musk have expressed concerns over advances in
AI leading to human extinction" (Zola, 2021).

O'Gieblyn, says in her article that "many transhumanists, such as Kurzweil, contend that they are carrying on
the legacy of the Enlightenment", which, as I mentioned,
was an era that laid the foundation for a scientific, rather than religious worldview. She goes on to say that she
"learned that most transhumanists are atheists who, if
they engage at all with monotheistic faith, defer to the
familiar antagonisms between science and religion." So,
does this mean that transhumanists, like Kurzweil, who
feel they are carrying on the Enlightenment, want to lay
down a "scientific" worldview, not a religious one, and
perhaps this epoch of our modern day, Great Awakening,
is about a spiritual battle we are fighting between man

and God?

Of course, that battle has been playing out for centuries, but not like it's playing out now. Like I said, perhaps we were born to be here, at this exact time, because this spiritual battle is going to have us figuring out one of the most complex, existential, as well as ethical puzzles ever created by man. O'Gieblyn, contends, in her article, that "although few transhumanists would likely admit it, their theories about the future are a secular outgrowth of Christian eschatology", which is "the part of theology concerned with death, judgment, and the final destiny of the soul and of mankind." Does that mean, from a transhumanist's perspective, the way death is dealt with is to transform us into what Kurzweil calls "spiritual machines, where we would transfer or 'resurrect' our minds onto supercomputers, allowing us to live forever?" O'Gieblyn mentions that "transhumanists today wield enormous power in Silicon Valley. Entrepreneurs like Elon Musk and Peter Theil, billionaire, co-founder of PayPal, and first outside investor of Facebook, identify as 'believers', where they have founded thinktanks such as the Singularity and the Future of Humanity Institute", and that "the movement are no longer abstract theoretical musings, but are being embedded into emerging technologies at organizations such as Google, Apple, Tesla and SpaceX." It's interesting that Musk is a "believer", even though he has expressed his concerns about "advances in AI leading to human extinction."

I don't know about you, but I don't feel comfortable with these transhumanists, deciding the future of humanity for us. O'Gieblyn says in her astute article that "losing faith in God in the 21st century is an anachronistic experience, and that you end up contending with the kinds of things the west dealt with more than a hundred years ago: materialism, the end of history, the death of a soul."

I ask you this. What is the initiation into this Great Awakening of our time, and who is ready to be initiated? Apparently, hardcore transhumanists do not believe in the existence of a soul, and consider themselves atheists, so let me ask you another important question. If there was a requirement that to be a part of the Great Awakening, and future of our humanity, you had to relinquish your soul, would you? I mean, if you believe that we will be transformed into what Kurzweil calls "spiritual machines, where we would transfer or 'resurrect' our minds onto supercomputers, allowing us to live forever", there is no need for a soul, correct? And, if you go by World Economic Forum, founder, Klaus Schwab's belief that you will "own nothing, have no privacy, and life will never be better" (Auken 2016), if I get this all correct, it sounds like you will be soulless, and absolutely miserable.

Dear friends, can you now see why it is time to awaken? To be a part of the Great Awakening of our time is to fight for your soul to exist, and whether you believe in a God, or not, please believe in something, other than transforming yourself into a machine. Of course, we would all love to live forever, but not by "resurrecting" our minds onto supercomputers!

Your greatest initiation into the Great Awakening is not to fear death, but trust that your soul is eternal. Resurrecting our minds onto supercomputers, as these transhumanists want us to do, is not how we will live forever!

Let Sufi poet, Rumi, remind us of what it means to be human:

"I died as mineral and became a plant, I died as plant and rose to animal, I died as animal and I was human, Why should I fear? When was I less by dying? Yet once more I shall die human, To soar with angels blessed above. And when I sacrifice my angel soul I shall become what no mind ever conceived. As a human, I will die once more, Reborn, I will with the angels soar. And when I let my angel body go, I shall be more than mortal mind can know."

CHAPTER 14

Staying On The Path Of Awakening

The path of awakening is not becoming who you are. Rather it is about becoming who you are not.

- ALBERT SCHWEITZER

If you find yourself on the path of awakening, how do you stay on it? The difficulty lies in weakening to life's trials and tribulations, and there will be many, especially if you walk the spiritual path of the divine warrior. The journey to awaken is one of profound initiation, and as I spoke about in the previous chapter, your initiation is not to fear death, but trust that your soul is eternal.

Man will grapple with his soul, time and time again, especially now, when we are facing the dangers of things like transhumanism, which seems to negate the soul, if we are aspiring to replace ourselves with machines. This includes the issue of global governance, which can make, monitor, and enforce rules on us that go against our civil liberties and freedoms. Our soul knows when it is being oppressed or manipulated, and we must fight against whatever endangers it. As French general, Ferdinand Foch said, "The most powerful weapon on earth is the human soul on fire."

Addressing the imminent threats to our humanness, our soul – the very core of our being, should be on everyone's mind, but it is not. Again, it is those that are truly awake, who know about the threats we are facing, and have courageously faced them at a time of intense polarization by those who wish, or refuse, to accept what is happening, right under our noses. I can assure you that you will not hear about what I'm bringing to your attention on your nightly news. Most, if not all news media is biased, in some way, so listening to your favorite news channel will only reinforce what you already believe, as if there is nothing to be concerned about, other than what you are being told to be concerned about (mostly, the next virus). What I can say to that is, I'm concerned about you not knowing what all of us should be concerned about at this time, and there is plenty to be concerned about.

It truly boggles my mind that talking about anything that goes against the mainstream (media) narratives, is immediately categorized as alarmist, or again, a conspiracy theory. People who refuse to believe what's going on, other than what they're told by their news of choice, our government, and health officials, act like you're talking about UFOs and extra-terrestrials, which, ironically, occasionally gets slipped on the news, as if to take the attention off the very things we should be putting our attention on (I suggest watching the movie, *Wag The Dog*, to see how easy it is for the media to quell a situation by fabricating something else to grab our attention). Yes, life does imitate art, or is it the other way around?

It will be challenging, at times, to stay on the path of awakening, especially when you feel that the world has slipped into what Dr. Robert Malone calls, "mass formation psychosis", which I mentioned earlier, and why he, and psychologist Mattias Desmet, use it to explain why it appears as if millions of people have gone into a mass hypnosis, completely losing their critical thinking skills, and readily accepting the Covid-19 narrative without questioning the safety and efficacy of the vaccines. I know that for those of us who chose to be awake these last two years, it wasn't easy, and at times, it was even grueling. We made it our business to watch endless videos, or listen to podcasts of some of the most courageous doctors, scientists, and thought leaders who spoke out against the tyranny we are facing, and read everything we could possibly find by doctors (you may not know about because of the heavy censorship and cancel-culture), who felt, in good conscience, the need to speak up about things like vaccine injuries and deaths due to the Covid-19 experimental shot. At times, I would cry myself to sleep, knowing that extremely important information was being withheld from the public, and constantly being disregarding as "misinformation." It was especially hard when some of my loved ones and friends just weren't seeing it, and the more you tried to convince them to wake up, the more they thought you were being "overly dramatic" or "too passionate" or again, a "conspiracy theorist." I believe in Karma, and I have no doubt that the truth will prevail, and all those who were complicit in covering up the truth, will be held accountable. They have participated in Crimes Against Humanity (Bill Gates, and Anthony Fauci are at the top of the list), to the likes of which we have not seen since World War II. Again, please listen to people like Robert. F. Kennedy Jr., and German lawyer, Rainer Füllmich, who is suing the World Health Organization ("The Corona Scandal" n.d.), because he believes that leaders and health authorities around the world have misled the public about the seriousness of the Covid-19 epidemic (he has also been heavily censored).

I don't care if you think what I am saying is alarmist. What I do care about is if you refuse to see or accept any of this as true. If you are doubting anything of what I have written thus far, and certainly have a right to, I suggest you do your own due diligence to see if any of it is true (and that does not mean only relying on your biased news sources). Please go outside your comfort zone, or political leanings, and expand your source(s) of information as much as you possibly can. I gave you a list of suggestions of who to listen to, watch, or read, in Chapter 3 - What You Need To Know About Awakening. Please listen to as many of them as you can, and before you rush to judgment, honestly ask yourself if any of what they are saying, or proposing, does not provoke curiosity in you, or make you at least consider a different point of view other than the one you held so tightly over the last two years because you were told to, or felt you had to, to stay alive.

For those of you who know all of this (and perhaps more than I do), I commend you for going down as many rabbit holes as you needed to, in order to find out more than what was told to us. I find the proverb, "He who asks questions is a fool for five minutes. He who does not ask questions remains a fool forever", quite true. So many of you brave warriors asked questions every-step of the way, and I have no doubt, you were made to feel the fool many times, even shamed. And worse, there were people who were made to feel as if they were some kind of leper, and were not invited (or uninvited) to weddings and baby showers of dear (some of them lifelong) friends who judged them harshly for honoring their bodily autonomy, and chose not to get the Covid-19 experimental shot; even if it was because they had a compromised immune system, or underlying health condition. And how about hearing people (including actress Jennifer Aniston) out of ignorance say, "I will not associate, or be friends with anyone who has not gotten the Covid-19 shot" (Reuters 2021). It got so crazy that, even if you got the shot, but refused the booster (or ongoing boosters), there were those people who still felt that they did not want to associate or be friends with you because you weren't "fully vaccinated" (be prepared to lose friends if you refuse to get every booster that comes up). I don't recall anyone who chose not to get the Covid-19 experimental shot, say any of that type of nonsense. They were accepting of whatever others chose to do, and didn't exclude, or uninvite someone from their home, or an event they were having because they got the shot. I will also say that what children were put through, who did not receive the experimental Covid-19 shot, some because of underlying health issues, or family religious beliefs, was unconscionable. Many of them were shamed by their teachers, bullied by their classmates, and some schools even went as far as to make unvaccinated children eat their lunches isolated outside of the school, in freezing weather. The psychological damage from this could be irreparable, and many parents feel they will have their day in court suing the schools, teachers, administrators, and board members who were complicit.

If you're someone who did get the shot, and you don't already know this, there are those that believe (some of them are doctors, the one's unafraid to speak out), that if you did receive the Covid-19 experimental shot, you could spread something called "viral shedding" to those who have not received the shot. In an article in National Times Australia, "Pfizer Confirms Covid-19 Vaccinated People Can 'Shed' Spike Proteins And Harm The Unvaccinated", it says that "a new study has confirmed that people who have been vaccinated against Covid-19 produce excessive spike proteins that are capable of passing the Blood Bain Barrier causing irreparable damage to the brain – and Pfizer's own documents warn that vaccinated people actually shed these excessive spike proteins putting the unvaccinated at risk for harm" (National-Times-Australia 2021).

In another article, in Children's Hospital of Philadelphia, "Viral Shedding and Covid-19: What Can and Cannot Happen," it explains that "viral shedding can occur following vaccination if the vaccine contains live, weakened viruses because that type of vaccine causes immunity through viral reproduction" (Philadelphia 2021). This particular article, which I find biased, states that "the new Covid-19 vaccines being used in the U.S. do not contain live virus, so they are not capable of causing shedding." Apparently, the Johnson & Johnson, and AstraZeneka vaccines are considered live vaccines because they both contain adenovirus. But, according to another (biased) article in Nebraska Medicine "Covid-19

Vaccines, irregular periods and spike protein shedding", it claims that "the adenovirus in both the Johnson & Johnson and AstraZeneka vaccines can't replicate so there's no way they can shed" ("COVID-19" 2021). Are either of those pharmaceutical companies willing to come forward and prove that isn't true? Keep in mind, they don't have to prove anything to anyone who gets one of their vaccines, or be liable if anyone gets injured or dies.

Many women have reported on social media about their menstrual changes (and many were censored), like experiencing heavier bleeding than normal, and early and late periods after receiving the Covid-19 shot, but again, these reports are either being minimized by doctors (the ones who also feel that pregnant women should get the Covid-19 vaccine), even though in an article in The New York Times, "Pregnant Women Get Conflicting Advice on Covid-19 Vaccines", it says that, "experts partly blame a lack of data because expectant mothers have been excluded from clinical trials" (Mandavilli and Rabin 2021), but they should be the guinea pigs for this experimental vaccine while they're carrying a baby, hopefully, to full term? So much of this alarming information, was, and continues to be debunked by researchers that claim these reports only represent "a small portion of vaccinated women", according to the National Institutes of Health. And, most of the articles written about any of this are being targeted as "misinformation" because the "fact checkers" reign supreme on being the judges of misinformation about anything that opposes their narratives. So, if you look up anything that questions the authorities who establish which narrative you must follow, you may as well just throw your arms up and admit that you are, indeed, a conspiracy theorist! If you're comfortable with that, let's move on.

If you are someone who missed barbeques, showers, weddings, graduations, or any event that you were excluded from because you did not get the Covid-19 experimental shot, I'm sure that felt really crummy. But, the good news is that if you have chosen the path of spiritual growth, you have some wisdom, and know that everyone is on their life journey at a level of understanding and maturity, they are capable of being on, and not to judge them harshly because of it. There are the judges, and the judged, in this pandemic drama, but ultimately, at the end (if there is an end to this madness), eventually, each one of us will face our maker and be judged according to how we lived and behaved. Was it morally and honorably, as the Eightfold Noble Truths, asks of us, or did we feel superior to others, or more entitled? This pandemic has created something that could best be described as some kind of medical caste system, and clearly, it has pitted people against one another in ways that is anything but spiritually conscious.

The best way that you can stay on the path of awakening, is to simply keep yourself as awake and aware as you possibly can. And one of the most noble things you can do, is stay committed to your spiritual growth, daily. It truly is an honorable path to be on, and when you face obstacles, judgment, ridicule, or anything that feels another person is not seeing your Buddha nature, which in Buddhism means that all humans have the nature of Buddha within them already, and like a seed, we have the potential to grow, and become enlightened like the Buddha; just know that if they don't see that, do not take it personally. Instead, smile at them, and feel love and compassion in your heart.

That is what will save our humanity. Love and compassion.

CHAPTER 15

How Awakening Will Change Your Life

He who is free in the body, but bound in the soul is a slave; but on the contrary he who is bound in the body, but free in the soul, is truly free.

- EPICTETUS

There is a story about Jesus that when he healed a blind man, he asked him, "Do you see anything?" The man replied, "I see men as trees walking." He could see, but he was confused. Jesus touched his eyes again; then he saw clearly; he had not only sight, but insight, to make sense of what he saw" (Mark 8:22-26).

That story is relevant to this chapter because one of the ways awakening will change your life is that you will see much more clearly, and, like the blind man, you will have not only sight, but insight, to make sense of what you see. Henry David Thoreau's quote also says it well, "It's not what you look at that matters, it's what you see." In my book, *Mindfulness and Mysticism*, I talk about lifting the veils of illusion, and seeing beyond the first layer of truth, which there are many. The veils of illusion, means there is much that is shrouded, and hidden from us, and to be a good veil lifter, you must go beyond what is presented, or told to you, again and again, until the truth is revealed for what it really is. Awakening is hard work, and for those who don't want to know what is true because it's too difficult to see, they choose the path of least resistance. Who wouldn't want to walk the path that doesn't require much of us, or shields us from knowing what can be unpleasant, even unbearable? Life may seem easier if you avoid knowing what's hidden behind the veils of illusion, but eventually, you will have to face what you avoided, or allowed yourself to believe because the truth does catch up to all of us, and as writer, Philip K. Dick said, "Reality denied comes back to haunt."

This time of the Great Awakening, will reveal those who either want to lift every veil of illusion they see, or those who will continue to deny, even protect the deceptions to keep life going as they want it to. But, if we honor, and live by the first Noble Truth of the Eightfold path - Right View, it is the most significant first step on the path of awakening, and means that we see the world and everything in it as it really is, not as we believe, or want it to be.

Your life will be deeply changed by walking the "Right View" path, and, may at times, feel lonely, but the truth is, there are millions of people all over the world who are walking the path of awakening, and with time, more will awaken. It is the awakened souls who will walk this earth as it was intended to be — heaven on earth, and as Thoreau said, "There is only one path to heaven. On earth, we call it love." The awakened ones know that love is the only path to be on. It is the truth of all truths, and if you see the lies and deception that are all around us, you will also have the insight to know that the number one thing we are being manipulated to believe, is not to love one another, despite our differences. If anything, during the pandemic, we were encouraged to judge each other harshly, even rat someone out, if they didn't go along with what the authorities were telling us to do. Where is love in that, I ask you? And where is love in excluding people to gather, and break bread with, because they believe in bodily autonomy, or self-sovereignty?

How unthinkable, that even at places of worship, some clergy members would separate their congregation from the vaxed, and what was being called, "anti-vaxxers." Were those people who were being called anti-vaxxers against you, or were they opposing the will of others to control them? Was that what God would want people to do in places of worship? To separate, segregate, and not hold love in our hearts for others who are following their hearts to decide what feels real, and most right, for them? We must trust that they are following their Noble Truth of Right View, and we cannot impose our view onto them.

Yes, dear reader, you will feel many changes on this spiritual path you have wisely chosen. And, at times, it might leave you feeling sorrow in your heart for those who are choosing not to awaken. Be strong and vigilant in your commitment to this path of awakening because it is people like you who will lead us to the new world, and it will not be a new world "ordered" by those who do not hold love in their hearts, and feel that man is destined to be programmed as a machine, to stay eternal. We cannot give up, not even for a moment, our Right View that love is what will keep our humanity going, and anyone who tells us otherwise is not connected to divine love in their own heart. We can try to help them awaken, in hopes they will see that this Great Awakening we are in the midst of, is intended to wake up everyone, but only those that choose to awaken with us, will.

Yes, "There is only one path to heaven", and the awakened ones know, "on earth, we call it love."

CHAPTER 16

Your Relationships As You Awaken

Ask the universe to help you meet your soul tribe.
Find your people so that you have the support and
love you deserve. Connect and grow with other
awakened souls.

- ANONYMOUS

Lies don't end relationships.
Usually, the truth does...

- ANONYMOUS

More relationships ended during the last two years, and many of those relationships were dearly valued. The reason why so many of those relationships and friendships came to an end, was that many people felt they could not agree on opinions and decisions during the pandemic, and they had no choice but to move on from a friendship, or even cut a family member out of their life.

This seems so extreme, to end a friendship, or be estranged from a family member because you can't agree on opinions or beliefs, but as it's been said, these are "unprecedented times", so decisions that were made about our relationships took on a whole new meaning, and it was unlike anything we had experienced before. As I mentioned earlier, people were so diametrically opposed in their viewpoints about the pandemic, the vaccine, and the mandates, it created terrible dissent and polarization, which many relationships and friendships just couldn't survive. But one of the main reasons that many people felt they had to end a relationship (or more than one), was because there was something deep that was changing in them, which I have called the "Great Awakening", and they could not hold themselves back from heeding the call that was driving them to be on the path of spiritual growth, to fully awaken.

Not everyone is on the same spiritual path at the same time, and for some people, they are not on any type of spiritual path at all. That is what is most noticeable to anyone who has embarked on the path of awakening, and why many of them feel that nothing can stop them from continuing their path of transformation, which they also feel is the most important path to be on at this time. This feeling to awaken is so powerful, that for those who have embarked on the spiritual journey to raise their consciousness beyond the dense layer most people live on, many of them say it is the path they were born to take, and you either know this about yourself, or you don't. So, why is it that some people know this about themselves, and others do not? There are different theories as to why some people are spiritual, and others aren't. One of them is the evolution of our soul's spiritual timeline — meaning that we are at different points in our spiritual growth, and some people are further along. Another theory is that some people are "new souls" and others, "old souls". What that means is newer souls want to live life more superficially, or hedonistically, and are more interested or preoccupied with things that give them pleasure, physically and materialistically. And the older souls want to go into the depths of life and learn all that they can about what they are doing here on this earth, therefore, drawn to feed their spirit more than just their physical desires.

So, maybe you consider yourself an old soul, if you find yourself drawn to spiritual growth, and feel a deep desire to go further on your spiritual path of awakening. And, if you feel that you are a new soul, perhaps you have a yearning to begin your spiritual path of awakening and are ready to. The beauty of the path of awakening is that you can begin it at any time in your life, and the sooner you do it, the better. The reason for that, I feel, is that if you think of awakening as an opportunity to have a deeper understanding of the universe, and your relationship with the spiritual world, it gives you a more conscious awareness of the world you inhabit, and your role in it. And wouldn't you want to know that sooner, rather than later, or at the end of your life?

Spirituality, as I said, concerns itself with matters of the spirit, as opposed to being preoccupied with our survival needs, which is something that most human beings are concerned about. Those needs are what evokes fear rather than acceptance or compassion, which is why whenever there is a serious situation, crisis, or something like a pandemic, people that are more concerned about their survival, will not be the ones thinking about their spirit, or the evolution of it. Bottom line is, anything that does not address survival, or avoiding death at all costs, is something those people have absolutely no interest in. But, if you're someone who happens to feel the complete opposite, and trust that every single thing you go through on this life journey, including getting a virus, a pandemic, or even facing the possibility of dying, is something to learn from, you will address it with a more conscious awareness, rather than from a place of fear.

Whether you're an old soul, or a new one, anyone can be on the spiritual path of awakening, you simply have to want to. I would think that you would get to the point where you're tired of living in fear most of the time, and constantly thinking about whether you're going to beat a virus or not, and possibly die. That fear has preoccupied millions of people's minds for more than two years, and how much longer do we want to live in fear over that? I'm not suggesting that we should just be passive and feel like, "hey, so if I get Covid-19 (or whatever variant comes down the pike) and die, so be it." That's not what I am saying at all. What I am saying is that living in fear constantly, and it being fueled by the government, health organizations, and the media, to keep us in a constant state of fear, is something you might want to consider seriously thinking about how much longer you want to live that way, as it is robbing you of precious moments to enjoy, and be grateful for.

And that is what will affect our relationships the most, how we choose to live. If you are someone who is not ruled by fear, and accepting and trusting of life in a way that makes you feel more connected to spirituality, you are likely someone who feels connected to something greater than "oneself", and have a sense of awe and reverence for the mystery of life, or what can also be called the cosmic laws of our expanding universe. These cosmic laws, which I also call sacred truths, basically means that all beings have equal rights to live on this planet to develop spiritually so that we can understand humanity's place in the universe. I highly doubt that wars, conflicts, hate, and violence, are in harmony with these cosmic laws, and until we awaken, we will be caught in the endless drama of our survival needs, and continue to place value on that, rather than the wellbeing of all sentient beings on this earth.

If you are someone who craves spiritual meaning, and feels that you are here on this earth plane — the greatest life school there is, and incarnated here at this exact time to know the sacred truths of the universe before your spirit leaves your body, the vessel it chose to inhabit, you will find yourself wanting to share this understanding with others who feel as you do. This isn't about all of us needing to agree, this is about honoring why we elected to incarnate into this life, and supporting each other on this miraculous, mysterious journey. There are millions of you all over the world who are on this spiritual journey in a similar way, and you will seek one another out, and build communities of like-minded people. This is an extraordinary time to be alive. Yes, it is challenging, but would you prefer not being here at this time? You are here, so let's continue to awaken, and direct this starship toward Our New World that we are creating together.

And keep in mind what astronomer and cosmologist, Carl Sagan said, "The significance of our lives and our fragile planet is determined only by our own wisdom and courage. We are the custodians of life's meaning. We long for a parent to care for us, to forgive us our errors, to save us from our childish mistakes. But knowledge is preferable to ignorance. Better by far to embrace the hard truth than a reassuring fable. If we crave some cosmic purpose, then let us find ourselves a worthy goal."

CHAPTER 17

Defining Your Purpose As You Awaken

The purpose of life is not to be happy. It is to be useful, to be honorable, to be compassionate, to have it make some difference that you have lived and lived well.

- RALPH WALDO EMERSON

In part of Carl Sagan's quote that I shared in the previous chapter, he says, "If we crave some cosmic purpose, then let us find ourselves a worthy goal." I interpret that as, if we have a powerful desire to know what the purpose of life is, we must acknowledge that our existence is connected to a greater purpose, which each of us is a part of. We are "the custodians of life's meaning", as Sagan's quote also says, which means that we are all responsible for what happens to this "fragile earth", as he calls it.

Defining our purpose begins with consciously participating in the well-being of this earth by thinking of ourselves as guardians of it. We are the caretakers, the protectors of this planet we inhabit, and the only way for us to steward its evolution successfully, is to be fully awake on the spiritual path. Each of us must ask ourselves what our purpose on the path of awakening is, and how can we best fulfill that purpose for the well-being of ourselves, and all sentient beings. This might sound like a lofty ideal, but why be on the path of awakening unless you have a desire to live nobly, and be of service in some way that can raise the consciousness on the planet. I think we have lost our way on the spiritual path, which is why I shared the Eightfold Noble Truths, in hopes that we can remind ourselves of what it means to live with moral principles, and be courageous and brave about saving our humanity, which it is in much need of.

It is you that must define what your purpose is on the path of awakening, and even if at times you feel very challenged, the very thing that should inspire you to continue on, is that the sacred truths of the universe await you to discover them, and once you do, you will be completely set free from the fear that controls your mind. When our purpose is combined with fearlessness, there is nothing we cannot do. And, to live life not dominated by fear means we are primed to delve into the depths of the spiritual journey so that we can awaken in the most extraordinary way, and no longer believe we need anyone to tell us how to live or survive. Once we know this, we no longer will believe that our survival is constantly being threatened, which has been repeatedly told to us by the very people that are telling us what to do to stay alive. Do you not see how we have been manipulated to believe we need people in power to keep us safe and alive? What is this childish need to be governed, even controlled, as if we need parenting? It is here in Sagan's quote, "We long for a parent to care for us, to forgive us our errors, to save us from our childish mistakes." And we will keep making our childish mistakes unless we individuate from our controllers — those that are keeping us ignorant. "But knowledge is preferable to ignorance", Sagan goes on to say. "Better by far to embrace the hard truth than a reassuring fable."

Our purpose on the path of awakening is to "embrace the hard truth" that we have been asleep far too long, and now we must do whatever we can to wake up and help change the trajectory that this planet is on. What greater purpose is there than to be a part of the Great Awakening and know that you are having a significant impact on our evolution, individually, and collectively. We are not meant to just coast through life, and feed off this earth, as if we are entitled to selfishly take, and not be generous of spirit, and give back. And that is why we must feed our spirit, first and foremost, because it needs to replenish this earth, and breathe life into its spirit too.

We all have a very important role in the Great Awakening, which is why it is so crucial for each of us to wake up from the slumber we have been in. We have a tremendous opportunity to do things very differently now, and return to the land to help it be more sustainable, which is why many people are learning how to farm, and grow their own food. We must also help protect the farmers, who are growing organic food, and providing it for us at our local farmer's markets. Be aware of the power grabbers who are trying to take their farmland away and buying acres of land all around. Today, Bill Gates owns the majority of America's farmland (242,000 acres) in 19 states. In addition, he owns 25,750 acres of traditional land and 1,234 acres of recreational land for total land holdings of 268,984 (Bauer 2021). Please do your research and connect the dots. Someone like Bill Gates, who suddenly has tremendous power over our health, and seems obsessed with vaccines — telling people what they should put in their bodies (he and Melinda Gates are the biggest donors to the WHO), is now buying up a tremendous amount of farmland, and he says it's not about climate. Is it for some altruistic reason to help the local farmers who work so damn hard, and support us getting healthy food delivered to our farmers markets, or grocery stores? I don't think so. I must mention that

Bill Gates is one of the high-ranked billionaires who has already invested $75 million in Impossible Foods, which on the surface appears like a vegetarian option as a way to eat, and help reduce pollution, but in truth, is genetically modified fake meat. I recommend reading, "Bill Gates: Let them Eat Fake Meat!" an article in the Defender by Children's Health Defense. Here is another example of how billionaires and technocrats are taking over everything from our health, to controlling our food sources and supply chains. Again, please do your research. It is incumbent upon each of us to get correct information and become more knowledgeable.

As Carl Sagan said so aptly, "Knowledge is preferable to ignorance."

CHAPTER 18

Your Role On
The Awakened Journey

Our consciousness is our contribution to reality.
What we perceive as real, becomes real.

- DEEPAK CHOPRA

Not everyone looks at their role in life as making a significant difference in the world. But I think we should ask ourselves why we believe you have to be someone like Gandhi, Mother Theresa, Martin Luther King, Jr., Nelson Mandela, even Jesus Christ, to change the world for the better, but since we are not the type of humanitarian leaders they were, we cannot. If we live life implementing something like the Eightfold Noble Truths, which Buddha set into motion to overcome ignorance, and be on the path of enlightenment, then each one of us is a leader in the making and can change the world in some way. Something like raising our consciousness can help change the world. You might not think that is significant on a grand scale, but if every single person on the planet had the intention to awaken and become more aware of how we can make a difference in the world, then that is what we would put into motion, and "our consciousness" will be "our contribution to reality", as Deepak Chopra says.

Who you are on the awakened journey will determine your role in society, and whatever intentions you set forward will make a difference in what can help change the world. That means every word, deed, and action, has an impact, and reverberates outward, wide, and far. Those great souls that I mentioned, like Gandhi, Mother Theresa, Martin Luther King, Jr., Nelson Mandela, and Jesus Christ, were very mindful human beings, and conscious of the well-being of others. They were in service to humanity, and people who were in their presence felt that there was something unique, and special about them, which was their consciousness vibrating on a high frequency because their souls were ignited to love and protect all sentient beings. At a time when the soul is being undervalued, and there is a desire to give our power over to AI, to have the ultimate power over human beings, we are heading towards a soulless world, if we are not careful, which is why it is so extremely important for us to define our role as "soulful" leaders on the awakened journey.

Maybe you haven't thought of yourself as a leader before, but I highly encourage you to change that perception of yourself. We need very awake and aware leaders now more than ever before. What we are witnessing at this time of our Great Awakening, are leaders who are more interested in power than caring about our wellbeing, or genuinely wanting to help change the world for the better. All you must do is look at how things are playing out all over the world, and ask yourself if you feel that the leader of your country is doing a great job in their leadership, and where, exactly, are they leading you to? Do we wait for someone like Martin Luther King, Jr., or Nelson Mandela to stand up for human rights and non-violence, while we stand by hoping that someone like them will "lead us to the Promised Land", a place of great happiness?

I think not. There is an urgent need for us to awaken, and I cannot stress strongly enough how important it is for each of us to heed the call to awaken now. Know that you have an extremely important role in this Great Awakening, and please do all that you can to keep yourself focused on where you would like to see us go. Yes, have a vision like the great leaders had. Be the visionary, the architect of change, and each day that you are out in the world, let people feel your unique presence, and the high frequency of your vibration.

"Vibrate at the highest frequency possible."

— Unknown

CHAPTER 19

What Being Awake Does For Humanity

You must not lose faith in humanity. Humanity is
an ocean; if a few drops of the ocean are dirty,
the ocean does not become dirty.

- MAHATMA GANDHI

Love and compassion are necessities, not luxuries.
Without them humanity cannot survive.

- DALAI LAMA

The sole meaning of life is to serve humanity.

- LEO TOLSTOY

How can we best serve humanity? Without question, it is to be awake. We will never be able to create the new world for ourselves that is free of greed, malice, hatred, deception, delusion, violence, and all of the other negative things that are dragging us down into chaos and destructivity, unless we wake up and realize that we must stop contributing to the erosion of our humanity, and do all that we can to protect it, before it's too late.

We are at a very pivotal time. Unless we regard this time as a Great Awakening and recognize the spiritual shift, we need to be a part of, I cannot say with certainty that our humanity will survive. I have always thought of myself as a perennial optimist, but the last few years opened my eyes in such a way that I have become more of a realist. I am unafraid to see things for what they truly are, as hard as that has been, and if having "Right View" is the very first step of the Noble Eightfold Truths to get us started on the path of living without ignorance, and seeing things for what they truly are, then I pray that as many people as possible, take that first step, immediately. Our humanity is screaming out to us. It needs our help, desperately. Can you not see that? How can we talk about things like transhumanism, artificial intelligence, micro-chips, a New World Order, and all the other eerie, sci-fi type changes that are quickly happening, and not think that we have taken a very scary turn on this planet?

It's not that I don't want to step into the future with

curious excitement and embrace the inevitable changes
that are happening, but not if the future imagined is dictated by a group of people who happen to be billionaires
and think they can mastermind our future for us. From
what we see so far, it is not looking like the type of future
we should be eager to accept. I suggest finding out who
the richest, most powerful people in the world are, and
I can assure you that they are designing the future they
want, and not the one we have in mind.

When you have someone like Ray Kurzweil, who is a
director of engineering at Google, and a leading advocate
of the transhumanism movement, say, "The 21st century
will be different. Soon we would reach the 'Singularity',
the point at which we would be transformed into 'Spiritual Machines'. We would transfer or 'resurrect' our minds
onto supercomputers, allowing us to live forever. Our
bodies would become incorruptible, immune to disease
and decay, and we would acquire knowledge by uploading it to our brains. Nanotechnology would allow us to
remake Earth into a terrestrial paradise, and then we
would migrate to space, terraforming other planets. Our
powers, in short, would be limitless" (Kurzweil 2001). It
really makes you wonder if something like this could be
the design of our future.

Why do I get the feeling that I am being subjected
to the dystopian fantasies of people like Kurzweil, Mark
Zuckerberg, Bill Gates, Klaus Schwab, and other men
who act like they have a type of God complex they feel

compelled to play out on all of us? I understand that there have been power hungry men who behaved like megalomaniacs since the beginning of time, but the crop of "technopreneurs" (an entrepreneur involved with high technology), who have become more visible, especially over the last few years, expressing their soulless, transhumanism "agendas" for us, makes me feel that we really are heading towards a type of "metaverse" they would love to seduce us in, with no way out. Even writing this, I find it very unsettling, but we mustn't be naïve to think that this type of future hasn't already arrived. If we don't quickly awaken, we will be led, instead of leading ourselves, right into a computer-generated virtual reality where our avatars will "do everything from buy land and host parties to even get married", as the Metaverse is already promising to do.

If we truly care about our humanity, we would be less concerned about living forever as supercomputers, but instead, living right now as awake, conscious human beings, who can direct ourselves towards a future that is benevolent, peaceful, and in harmony with nature. We really should ask ourselves, do we as human beings have a need to destroy what is good?

How can we not lose faith in humanity, which Gandhi, in his quote above, asks us not to. Our humanity is like "an ocean", as he so beautifully described it, but our human ocean seems quite dirty right now, and the only way the entire ocean will not become dirtier, is if we awaken to clean it.

CHAPTER 20

Living In
A Parallel Universe

There are many, many, many worlds
branching out at each moment you become aware
of your environment and then make a choice.

- KEVIN MICHEL

As more people are waking up, they are feeling like they are living in a parallel universe with those that are not. A parallel universe, also known as a "parallel dimension, alternate universe, or alternate reality, is a hypothetical self-contained plane of existence, co-existing with one's own" (Wikipedia Contributors 2019). This feeling of living in a parallel universe is more pronounced when you're speaking to someone about your awakening, and they have absolutely no idea what you're talking about. It's one thing when you're talking to someone who maybe you're not completely surprised they don't get it, but when you begin to share your perceptions and insights about the world, and how things are unfolding, with smart, intelligent people, and they are clueless about your observations, that's when you really feel that you are co-existing with them in this universe, along with their universe; meaning you are literally in two different universes at the same time. I say "this universe" for those who are awake because they don't feel the need to replace this universe with another one.

I know that sounds very sci-fi, but it seems that there are many things going on right now that feel as if we are living in a reality that contains science-fiction type elements, like advanced technology, and many other futuristic concepts. The fact that I'm writing about things like transhumanism, and artificial intelligence (AI), as a Mindfulness practitioner, it does make me feel that not only is there a spiritual shift happening, but there's also a shift in our perceptions of reality, and if you have an awareness of it, you can live in this multi-reality universe with equanimity and wisdom. The advantages of being awake are so multi-faceted, that you can think of it as being a chameleon who has a highly developed ability to change its color as a type of camouflage protection. I believe that those who are awake, have some extraordinary abilities that can rival the transhuman model of our future self. And, for all of those transhumanists who think that human beings becoming supercomputers is the big "wow", all I can say is, watch out for the awakened ones, for they are advancing their consciousness in ways I'm afraid you will be clueless about.

Advanced consciousness is the big "wow", as far as I'm concerned, and if you're not a part of the awakening movement, I'm afraid you will miss out on experiencing different levels of higher consciousness that I don't believe any machine will ever be able to do. Stripping away things like our soul, and human consciousness so that we can be eternal as a supercomputer, as many transhumanists long for, will tamper with our collective consciousness, which is a unifying force within society that is a moral and ethical consciousness we all share, and this will be extremely dangerous for our humanity, perhaps irreparable. There is a very loud message that transhumanists are sending out, and that is, we should prepare ourselves to eventually be replaced by computers and robots, and if you want to be a part of that universe, you can. They make it seem, as if, one day, we will be choosing our respective universes, and soon there might be advertisements promoting these new types of universes (like the Metaverse) for us to sign up for.

The problem for me with most transhumanists, that I am aware of, is that they don't seem to put value on advancing human consciousness because they are far too enamored with things like artificial intelligence, which are basically "computer systems that are able to perform tasks that normally require human intelligence" (Galimova et al. 2019). But artificial intelligence is not the natural intelligence that humans and animals have, so what will we do when humans will be taken over by robots without the natural intelligence that we have, and we will be living in an actual sci-fi reality where human consciousness no longer exists.

If you choose to be in this universe, as an awakened one, you will become even more aware that you are sharing a separate reality with others who are not awake, and it can feel like the world has literally changed into a science-fiction reality, as if overnight. I do consider that we are advancing in our evolution exponentially, and it seems that things have accelerated over the last few years when we were the most vulnerable, and susceptible to believing all sorts of things during the pandemic, which I find rather curious. If you are awake, I'm sure you can relate to how it is starting to feel like all of this is unfolding in a way, as if it has been planned with great, almost brilliant precision, and it seems that it has. Bill and Melinda Gates, in partnership with the John Hopkin's Center for Health Security, and the World Economic Forum Foundation, hosted a private meeting called "Event 201", which was a "high-level pandemic exercise" on October 18, 2019, in New York, just six weeks before the real

Covid-19 outbreak ("Event 201, a Pandemic Exercise to Illustrate Preparedness Efforts." 2019). And, supposedly, Bill Gates did not "predict" the Covid-19 outbreak when he backed the pandemic simulation. You must wonder about these types of strange coincidences, and use your intelligence to connect the dots in a way that makes sense, at a time when so much doesn't.

And that's exactly what awake people do. They connect the dots because that's what you do if you want to see the forest from the trees, and not be in total denial about what's staring us right in the face. Most people who are awake are completely stupefied by how so many people, at a time when there are so many strange coincidences going on, seem as if they are completely oblivious to connecting the dots, and if you were to say something to them like, "aren't you connecting the dots?", they would probably look at you with complete cluelessness, and say, "what dots?" This is the type of parallel universe I'm talking about. There are those who have looked at the events of the last few years very closely, connecting the dots along the way so they could make sense of all the strange, illogical things that were happening, and those who never connected a single dot because they never thought that anything that was happening was strange or illogical, so therefore, there was no need to connect the dots because there weren't any. And this goes back to awareness. When you are awake, you are aware of everything that is going on around you, and can see beyond the surface to recognize what is going on in your environment, as well as the interconnectedness of all things in the universe, so therefore, it's almost impossible not to connect the dots. As Thoreau said, "It's not what you look at that matters, it's what you see", and if you don't see the dots to connect, you are not seeing what is most important to see.

So, how do you live in this parallel universe, as an awake human being, with others who are not awake? If you hold the belief that we are living in a multi-reality universe, then maybe you just need to go about your business in your awakening and accept that there are other people you share this planet with who are going about their business staying unconscious. It's always going to be mind-boggling when you encounter those people (some of them might be in your life), and what is most noticeable about them is how unaware they are of the very things you are hyper aware of. It can feel as if there is a meteor heading towards the earth that you see, and they don't. I have no doubt there have been many times when you literally shook your head in disbelief over how unaware some people are of things that are going on right now that seem as if they're happening with bright, neon lights, or pyrotechnics, and they still are completely oblivious to it. But, not all the most important things that are happening right now, are blatantly obvious, which is why

I suggest being a good veil lifter, and that means, lifting back the veils of illusion.

Keep in mind that the pandemic simulation that Bill and Melinda Gates hosted at the World Economic Forum, was done behind closed doors, and only the richest and most powerful elites in the world were invited to be a part of it, which you and I would never know about, unless, again, we made it our business to know. Make it your business to know everything you possibly can in the days ahead, as the world will continue to change, ever so quickly. Choose to live fully awake, and you will be way ahead of this race to transcend human consciousness.

You, as an awakened one, will have complete awareness of your existence, and the ability to experience and feel your wakefulness. I doubt there will be supercomputers able to have that experience with you.

CHAPTER 21

A Conscious Civilization

Every civilization must contend with an unconscious
force which can block, betray, or countermand
almost any conscious intention of the collectivity.

- FRANK HERBERT

This race that I speak of to transcend human consciousness,
is a major threat to our civilization. If we don't work
together to maintain the moral and ethical consciousness
needed to unify, and hold together our collective consciousness, it will be commandeered by those who want to replace
it with artificial intelligence, transhumanism, and anything
else that can destroy our humanity. That means we will no
longer function as a cohesive, unified collective, existing
together for a common purpose to protect our humanity,
and once that happens, we no longer acknowledge the su-

preme soul of all, "Anima Mundi", which in Latin means "world soul". This is an intrinsic connection between all living beings, which relates to the world in much the same way as the soul is connected to the human body. If we don't acknowledge the world as a living, spiritual entity, and that there is a divine truth that energizes all life in the universe, we will have such little regard for our humanity and this planet, the way we will justify abandoning it, or even destroying it, is to think that creating something like Elon Musk's SpaceX, with the goal of enabling people to live on other planets, will be the solution. But how will we live on another planet, if we can't even successfully live on this one? Is having a futuristic fantasy that we should allow ourselves to be taken over by artificial intelligence, an indication that we're going to thrive on another planet as high functioning, albeit soulless human beings?

With all the extreme changes happening to our world right now, it isn't engendering much faith in how our future will look. I think we have the order of our spiritual evolution out of whack. Again, if there isn't an emphasis on the importance of self-realization, and a bypassing of doing the inner-work to awaken, we're just going to be in a hurry to find quick solutions for our man-made problems, like, produce experimental vaccines without proper clinical trials, pull out of a war-torn country quickly, like we did in Afghanistan, allow for the pharmaceutical industry to constantly bombard and poison us with the newest drugs that will keep us numb, anesthetized, or more sick; hurry along genetic engineering programs like Bill Gates is doing by investing in a veggie burger that "bleeds like beef" (Nickelsburg 2017), so what we eat, which will no longer be real, can be quickly produced for mass consumption. And, to add to that, Elon Musk's SpaceX program, that eagerly wants to get us off this planet and on to another one.

Better, faster, and more powerful, seems to be the mantra of our times, "thanks to a new partnership with SpaceX's Starlink satellite internet, with their 'Coverage Above and Beyond', setup, mobile phones could connect to satellites and use a slice of a connection providing around 2 to 4 Megabits per second connection (total) across a given coverage area" (Clark 2022). I mentioned the dangers of our advanced technology earlier, but with something like the SpaceX Starlink satellite internet, we must consider the dangers and risks of the technology we are creating, and there are serious concerns about 5G health risks." It is quite alarming to read in the article "5G Health Risks, The War Between Technology and Human Beings," that "over 180 scientists and doctors in almost 40 countries are warning the world about 5G health risks." These scientists' response was, "We, the undersigned scientists, recommend a moratorium on the roll-out of the fifth generation, 5G, until potential hazards for human health and the environment have been fully investigated by scientists independent from industry. 5G will substantially increase exposure to radio frequency electromagnetic fields (RF-EMF)…and has been proven to be harmful for humans and the environment" (Wagner, 2019).

We are such hurried, impatient people. All we want to do is get out of the moment we are in, so we can be in another moment we think will be better, faster, and more powerful. This is Mindfulness 101. To do the very opposite. We must learn, first, how to be in the very moment we are in and be as fully awake and aware in that moment as we possibly can. What we bring to that moment should be pure, conscious awareness, so that we can have a clear, untainted mind that functions from a moral and ethical understanding of what we are creating in each moment, and that goes for the 5G health concern, which should have been thought about very carefully by those who created it. It is from this pure consciousness, which Mindfulness helps us cultivate, we can not only think about what we are creating, but set our intention for it, responsibly, knowing that it can affect others, even the whole world. Mindfulness keeps you accountable and responsible for how you think, moment by moment, and creates a seamless awareness of every single thought that we have. Imagine the thoughts that occupy the minds of those who are creating such advanced, even dangerous technology, and that includes the minds of transhumanists. We know what is occupying their minds, and exactly what their intentions are. How can we be a conscious civilization, and

live good, civilized lives, if we can't even raise our consciousness in the moments of our lives? If we don't have
a conscious awareness of how we are participating in the
betterment of humanity, we are, whether we are aware of
it, or not, contributing to the decline of civilization. This
is how precise we must be in our individual consciousness,
which connects to a collective one.

I want you to think of yourself, for a moment, as an
architect of consciousness, which means that you are
fully aware of yourself, your environment, and everything
that is going on right now in the world and can oversee
how it's going. How do you perceive what is happening?
Does it seem positive, productive, and supportive of our
humanity and the planet? How would you like things
to be different, or better? There's so much talk about the
concern of our environment, and global warming. But
how much conscious awareness are we putting on things
like sustainability? It's so easy to blame big corporations
for the problems we're having, but what is each one of
us doing to change those problems in ways that we can?
I see more and more people returning to the land and
learning how to live more sustainably by growing their
own food. That's a perfect example of making a conscious
decision to "be the change we wish to see in the world",
that Gandhi spoke of, and we need to do more of that.
Instead of spending so much of our precious time wasting
it on not getting along because we have different opin-

ions over things like politics, or a pandemic, why don't
we pivot, and take our power back from the government,
health organizations, big pharma, and every other controlling system that has us dependent on it and causing us
to be polarized from one another. Why not productively
use our intelligence to think of how we can stop deplet-
ing our natural resources, and figure out genuine ways
to create an ecological balance, and true environmental
sustainability, not the ambiguous Sustainable Development Goals (SDG's, or Global Goals), that are part of
the 2030 Agenda the United Nations and global elites of
the WEF talk about. We must seriously question exactly
how they intend to "end poverty and hunger", or "help us
realize human rights for all", as Agenda 2030 seeks to do.
And how is it possible that "no one will be left behind", as
the UN pledges to do (Schwab 2016). Bill Gates proposes that "magic seeds" will be the answer to end poverty
and hunger, which is a type of seed that can be produced
by "breeding select varieties of a crop that researchers
believe can produce a hybrid crop" (also called a maize),
and "would be more resistant to hotter, drier climates"
(Gates n.d.). And how do you create this magic seed?
According to Gates, AI must come into the picture, as
to be expected, since "breeding the best crops has largely
been a slow, manual process conducted by a handful of
modern breeders", as Gates says, and in order to "speed
this plant breeding work up", one of the solutions is what

researchers call "predictive modeling", which is "artificial intelligence software that processes the genome sequences of crops along with environmental date". Sounds like the perfect solution when you think like a computer software programming guy. In the world hunger article, Gates also says, "farmers will need to plant even newer seeds as the environment changes in unpredictable ways" (Cohen 2021), spoken by the computer software man who wants to spray dust into the atmosphere to block the sun. The potential risks of solar engineering outweigh the positives, and some of those risks are, "devastating ecological consequences if we suddenly stop", and, "it may not solve some of the key problems with climate change — and could make some worse" (Yarlagadda 2021).

I must say that it is almost impossible to learn everything you can about Bill Gates without going down many troubling rabbit holes, but that's the only way you can be a good dot connector, as I spoke about earlier. For us to realize a conscious civilization, it is going to take a lot of work on our part, and to become as awake as you possibly can, you must be unafraid to find out ugly truths along the way, and there are many. I also know that most people don't want to see those ugly truths and will do all they can to avoid them. I think that has a lot to do with why millions of people didn't question the narrative about Covid and the pandemic, and when you challenged their beliefs around it, they just couldn't handle it, for fear that the truth could be ugly, and too much to bare. Well, it's time for us to see things for what they truly are, as difficult or ugly as it may be, or else our civilization just might not make it. We seem to be hanging by a thread right now, especially when we hear about Putin's nuclear threats to Ukraine, but the only way for us to strengthen that thread and turn it into iron, is for each one of us to awaken. As we know, many civilizations before us have fallen, like the Roman Empires. We know from history what caused some of those civilizations to collapse, like economic troubles, government corruption, political instability, and pure laziness and negligence of the people of that civilization. Do we see any similarities with our civilization?

The World Economic Forum thinks two of the main factors for a civilization to collapse are, "uncontrollable population" ("Even as Birth Rates Decline Overpopulation Remains a Global Challenge," 2018), and "climate change" ("This Is How Much People around the World Think Climate Change Is Impacting Their Lives," 2022), which everything from acne to gender-based violence, seems to be blamed on climate change lately (Hannam 2021). As far as the uncontrollable population problem the WEF seems to be concerned about, maybe they should ask their fellow global elite, Bill Gates, what he thinks about it. According to an article "The Gates Family, Eugenics and Covid-19," says "in 2010, the Bill & Melinda Gates Foundation purchased 500,000 shares in

Monsanto valued at more than $23 million. This is when it became abundantly clear that the so-called benevolent charity is up to something other than eradicating disease and feeding the world's poor" (Nash 2020). The article goes on to say, "the evidence that GMOs causes disease has been piling up for decades, as the list of countries banning their import and cultivation grows." Bill openly promotes GMOs as the "answer to world hunger", so then, GMOs, which have been proven to cause disease and kill people, is his answer to world hunger? I guess that's one way of controlling the population, but if you couple that with his magic seed plan to conquer world hunger, you can see how many confusing, and contradictory rabbit holes this takes you down. I think it's important to include what's also mentioned in The Gates Family article that Bill Gates' father, Bill Gates Sr., "served on the board of Planned Parenthood at its beginnings before it became a re-branded organization birthed out of the American Eugenics Society", which they link from an article in American Eugenics Society (1926-1972). Eugenics, for anyone who doesn't know, is "the study of how to arrange reproduction within a human population to increase the occurrence of heritable characteristics regarded as desirable. Developed largely by Sir Francis Galton as a method of improving the human race, eugenics was increasingly discredited as unscientific and racially biased during the 20th century, especially after the adoption of its doctrines by the Nazis in order to justify their treatment of Jews, disabled people, and other minority groups" ("Eugenics Definition - Google Search" n.d.).

In an article in National Library of Medicine, "The Politics of Population: Birth Control and the Eugenics Movement", it says, "The birth control movement and the population control movement became inseparable in people's minds during the early years of the birth control movement, led by Margaret Sanger" (Gordon 1974). Even with the recent Supreme Court decision to overturn Roe v. Wade, which created what has been called a "seismic" political and societal shift throughout the United States, there will be those who still hold the belief in, not only having the right to choose abortion, but that birth control and abortion are essential to control population growth, and the most desirous way to do so. Melinda Gates is one of those people who considers both "contraception-promotion and population control as arguably the single-most important part of her work" (Nash 2020). There has been speculation that the Gates have a population control agenda, and in an article "The Long, Strange History of Bill Gates Population Control Conspiracy Theories" it says, "In 2010, a former staffer with a government health initiative in Ghana made a shocking claim: a project partially funded by the Gates Foundation had tested the contraceptive Depo-Provera on unsuspecting villages in the remote region of Navrongo, as part of an illicit population experiment" (Joyce, 2020). It goes on to say, "the new narrative was that Gates was waging chemical warfare on poor women in a neocolonial effort to suppress African births." And in an article in the Annual Survey of International & Comparative Law, it leans heavily towards the population control theory about Bill Gates as being more real than conspiracy, when it says, "The Gates Foundation focuses on world health and population and high-lights its strategy of accelerating scientific discovery with reducing costs. Since the early 2000s, the Global Alliance for Vaccines and Immunizations (Gavi), Global Health Innovative Technology Fund and PATH, all heavily funded by the Gates Foundation, have been distributing vaccines and drugs to vulnerable populations in Africa and India. In 2010, the Gates Foundation funded experimental malaria and meningitis vaccine trials across Africa and HPV vaccine programs in India. All of these programs resulted in numerous deaths and injuries, with accounts of forced vaccinations and uninformed consent. Ultimately, these health campaigns, under the guise of saving lives, have relocated large scale clinical trials of untested or unapproved drugs to developing markets where administering drugs is less regulated and cheaper" (Ahmed 2017). These are very disturbing allegations. Time will tell, along with everything else that we are witnessing during this Great Awakening, who participated in Crimes Against Humanity, and who did all they could to resist it.

As I said earlier, if ever there was a time to be awake, it is now. We need to be very aware of "an unconscious force" that author Frank Herbert speaks of in his quote above, and that "every civilization must contend with an unconscious force which can block, betray, or counter-mand almost any conscious intention of the collectivity." Please wake up to all that is happening around us. The signs are there, if you choose to see them. Be a good veil lifter, my friend.

Let us become a conscious civilization. One, unlike any other, before it. We don't have to fall, but instead, can rise high in our collective consciousness to create a better world that is authentically sustainable.

CHAPTER 22

Is An Awakened World Possible?

If you want to awaken all of humanity, then awaken all of yourself. If you want to eliminate the suffering in the world, then eliminate all that is dark and negative in yourself. Truly, the greatest gift you have to give is that of your own self-transformation.

- LAO TZU

There is a legend of an ancient, lost civilization called Lemuria, that existed 14,000 years ago in the Southern Pacific, and the Lemurian people were believed to be highly evolved, intelligent, and very spiritual. The mystery and intrigue of Lemuria has been kept alive by philosophers, mystics, and futurists for a very long time, and even today, there are many people who still believe that this continent really did exist, and for some of them, they have a mystical connection to Lemuria, as if they lived once before, during that time.

There is something about imagining a world that we believe can be, or once was, better than the one we live in presently. It seems that many transhumanists are, in fact, imagining another world to live in that they think will be better than this one, but it doesn't appear to be the kind of civilization, like Lemuria, where people are evolved, intelligent, and spiritual. If Lemuria was the kind of civilization we aspired to be, it would be an awakened one, not a world that is run by computers, and artificial intelligence. Where did our imagining of a civilized world go so wrong? And when did we stop aspiring to be evolved, intelligent, and spiritual beings? I believe that our greatest challenge to protect our humanity at this historical time, is to awaken all of humanity, and as Lao Tzu says in his quote above, but for that to happen, you must "awaken all of yourself", first.

We will never realize an awakened world unless each of us is committed to awaken, and from what we can tell over the last few years, we are living in what I described as a "parallel universe", and our universe consists of people who are awake, and those who are not. I would like to think that the pandemic sparked a spiritual awakening, and for millions of people, it has. But there are billions of us who occupy this planet, and unless more people get sparked, spiritually, I'm afraid we won't wake up in time to see a better world, than the one that is declining now. I shall remain hopeful, and hold the possibility that as more people awaken, others will too. There is something called "spontaneous spiritual awakening", which is when someone has a sudden, non-dual merging (an experience of oneness, and non-separateness from anything or anyone), and they perceive reality in a complete, divine way, be it religious or spiritual. Perhaps that could happen if more people awaken, and with a shift in their consciousness, they energetically can help awaken others too. I do feel that there are more and more people on the path of awakening, and can only hope that you, dear reader, are also on this path. Think of the infinite possibilities of a world that truly can be extraordinary, and all that we can create together as a conscious collective. But, I must warn you again that there are those people who I have mentioned that have a very strong, and what I believe to be, sinister vision of what they want the new world to be, and, as I cautioned, it should not be called a "New World Order."

The vison for that new world, as I've talked about, is held by the World Economic Forum founder, Klaus Schwab, and the global elites who are going along with his vision that "a new world could emerge, the contours of which it is incumbent upon us to re-imagine and to re-draw" as he says ("COVID-19'S Legacy: This Is How to Get the Great Reset Right," n.d.). More of his vision for a new world is, "Ubiquitous, mobile supercomputing.

Intelligent robots. Self-driving cars. Neuro-technological brain enhancement. Genetic editing" (Schwab 2016). Apparently, Schwab is "convinced that we are at the beginning of a revolution that is fundamentally changing the way we live, work and relate to one another", and you can read all about it in his book, *The Fourth Industrial Revolution*. Klaus Schwab is a very rich, powerful man, as are the other global elites who are members, or "stake holders" as Schwab calls them, of the WEF.

How can our vision to awaken possibly compete with such a monolith as the World Economic Forum, and the global elites who have the means and power to intervene a spiritual awakening, because they are, as Frank Herbert said, the "force which can block, betray, or countermand almost any conscious intention of the collectivity"? I really don't think it's an exaggeration for me to say that we are in the midst of a spiritual war between good and evil. Please read what I took off the World Economic Forum website, and draw your own conclusions:

"Previous industrial revolutions liberated humankind from animal power, made mass production possible and brought digital capabilities to billions of people. This fourth Industrial Revolution is, however, fundamentally different. It is characterized by a range of new technologies that are fusing the physical, digital, and biological worlds, impacting all disciplines, economies and industries, and even challenging ideas about what it means to be human."

Okay, let me stop right there for a moment. "Challenging ideas about what it means to be human?" I don't know what your idea of what it means to be human is, but mine is to be conscious, spiritual, and have the ability to connect and commune with the sacred and divine to derive meaning and purpose, (let me go on to say), and have strengths of character like love, humility, compassion, forgiveness, kindness, and (yes, there is more), a life-affirming view of oneself and the world (yes, more), the ability to approach life with depth and intelligence, and to be able to problem solve and organize the life journey into a cohesive collective so that we are functioning as an awakened humanity to realize a better world for all sentient beings (forgive me if I left anything out).

What kind of power grabbing madness is going on with these people who think they can take us over with something that sounds like it's straight out of Dr. Evil's mouth, the antagonist in the *Austin Powers* film series, and call it a "New World Order"? And who, in their right mind, isn't going to read the plans for the New World Order, and think to themselves this is the closest thing we've seen to Hitler's vision for only "one power" (the racially best one), to attain "complete and uncontested supremacy." When you begin to redefine what it means to be a human being, and insist that it should be "characterized by a range of new technologies that are fusing the physical, digital, and biological worlds", then yes, you are not only challenging, but threatening "what it means to be human."

I truly hope this is "shaking you to awaken you" so you can realize what is really going on right now. Practice the Noble Truth of "Right View", and see the world and everything in it as it really is, not as we believe, or want it to be. I do believe that an awakened world is possible, but only if each one of us eliminates all that is dark and negative in ourselves, as Lao Tzu says, so that we can awaken, and awaken all of humanity.

CHAPTER 23

Awakening Has Already Begun

Awakening is dynamic. Constantly evolving in accordance with life's realities. Unfolding from ego-self to compassionate self. From enclosed self to open self. From foolish self to enlightened self.

- TAITETSU UNNO

O nce you awaken, you can never go back. You know that you have changed in a way that is perfectly timed for what you are facing, as difficult as that may be, and if you hadn't chosen to be as awake and aware as you are right now, you could very well be one of the sleepwalkers (or dare I say zombies), who are drifting along on this planet, and imagine all the mind-blowing things you would be missing.

And, this certainly has been a mind-blowing time, if you consider all of the crazy things that have happened over the last few years and continue to happen each day. I just love when my fellow awakened ones comment on social media (when they aren't censored or cancelled) about things that are completely illogical, like how it's perfectly normal for men to compete in women's sports. Men should not be competing in women's sports for the simple reason that they are biologically stronger than women, who have less total muscle mass than they do, and have something called "testosterone-induced muscular hypertrophy" (Sinha-Hikim et al. 2003). I've seen some awakened people who refuse to play along with what feels like daily media mind games, and point out how we are being manipulated to believe things that are just flat out not true. Biologically, men and women are different, period. Let me be clear. I have no problem if you identify as one or the other, but please stop pretending that men can have a period, or give birth, when they can't. What I would like to see, rather than insisting that a duck is not a duck, is explaining, especially to children, who are being exposed to all sorts of brainwashing (even at their schools), that if a man transitions to a woman, he will have the biology of a woman, so therefore can have a period, or give birth. No, that is not so. What we're seeing is, when a woman becomes a transgender man, it is because she is still biologically a woman and has a uterus, and she, who is now a he, is able to have a period and give birth. To run an ad from

Calvin Klein on Mother's Day (Rogers 2022), featuring a pregnant transgender man with a beard, and pretending that he is a man able to be pregnant (completely denying that it is a biological woman), is where the danger lies. Why not openly admit that it is a biological woman who is a transgender man, and that's why she (now he) is pregnant. This has nothing to do with that I agree with supporting "new families" in our society, but once you blur the lines of reality, and not acknowledge our differences; especially biological, this is what fuels different realities, and we will continue to live in a universe with multiple realities, and people who insist that their distorted reality is the only one there is.

We really must acknowledge this need that people seem to have to impose their reality (whatever that is in their minds) onto others who don't live in their distorted, or made-up reality, that has completely gotten out of control. It feels as if there is a type of collusion to go along with this distortion of reality, for fear of not being "politically correct", and as a result of that fear, we are being subjected to a type of collective craziness, which suddenly, is being backed and supported by people in positions of power. They too, are adopting this "woke" political correctness to advance their own agendas, and insisting that we should go along with whatever flavor of the moment madness we are being forced to believe is true, when we know deep in our gut, it is not. And that is what is happening in our awakening. We are becoming increasingly more aware of the manipulations, mind games, gas-lighting, and well-orchestrated plan (New World Order) that has suddenly reared its ugly head, and the only way to counter it being turned into a global reality, is to awaken, and I mean, each one of us. This is a serious call to action, and I hope that you hear the call, loud and clear.

Let me assure you that the awakening has already begun (for those of you who are genuinely worried about what has happened to our world, and all of the craziness we are witnessing), and the awakening is in full force. But the only way for us to overcome any plan, or should I say, this well-planned agenda that is being put into motion to take over and control us, is for this Great Awakening to grow so large, it cannot be denied, controlled, or stopped. I'm optimistic enough to say that once you have this many people (there are millions all over the world, and it's growing) who have taken the metaphoric "red pill" instead of the blue one so they can step out of the Matrix, which in our case, isn't a dystopian future, but a very shaky present reality, that if we don't act quickly to free ourselves from it, we will be stuck in some type of dystopian future that the transhumanists are aiming for us to be in. And, like in *The Matrix* movie, I believe that our bodies could be used in some way, just like the characters bodies were being used in *The Matrix* they were trapped in. What I mean by that is when you have a global "medical emergency", unlike anything we've seen before, and governments and health organizations mandate that everyone on the planet be injected with an experimental shot, of which we do not know what is in it (and won't know for another 55 years what's in the Pfizer shot), and being told that if we don't take it, our lifestyles and livelihood will be seriously threatened, you tell me that our bodies are not being used for an experimental drug that its only purpose is to protect us from a virus we are being warned, ad nauseum, could kill us. And yet, CDC director, Rochelle Walensky, finally admitted that it does not stop you from getting Covid, or transmitting it (Sunnucks, n.d.).

So why in the world is there an incessant need to get this experimental shot into every human being on the planet, with boosters still being pushed? If it does not seriously make you wonder why, I don't think you're a good candidate for awakening, but I will give you, dear reader, the benefit of the doubt, and assume that you are a good dot connector, and realize how many things don't add up, or make sense. I don't want to take you too far down the rabbit hole, although I'd like to, because this book would never end, but let me just say that something more than just a preventive vaccine, is being injected into people's bodies that some doctors who have been brave enough to research it, and even look at it under a microscope, are extremely concerned about. The Moderna vaccine was put on hold in Japan after a pharmacist found black particles in it, and 3,790 people had already received a shot from that batch (BBC News 2021). And if that doesn't give you reason for concern, in an article in the International Journal of Vaccine Theory, it says, "the exceptionally rapid movement of these vaccines through controlled trials and into mass deployment raises multiple safety concerns. In this review we first describe the technology underlying these vaccines in detail. We then review both components of and the intended biological response to these vaccines, including production of the spike protein itself, and their potential relationship to a wide range of both acute and long-term induced pathologies, such as blood disorders, neurodegenerative diseases and autoimmune diseases" (Seneff and Nigh 2021).

Even Dr. Robert Malone, who is an infectious disease researcher, and the inventor of the mRNA technology (in cells, mRNA uses the information in genes to create a blueprint for making proteins), and has dedicated his life to vaccines (it's ludicrous to call this man an "anti-vaxxer"), has suggested that, "the Pfizer and Moderna vaccines might actually make Covid-19 infections worse", according to an article in The Atlantic, "The Vaccine Scientist Spreading Vaccine Misinformation" (Bartlett 2021). The article refers to a conversation between Dr. Malone, and political strategist, Steve Bannon, and makes it very clear that even though Dr. Malone is the inventor of the mRNA technology, "the back-and-forth between

Bannon and Malone was premised on misinformation". Why is it that the conversation between Bannon, and the doctor who invented the technology that is used in both the Pfizer and Moderna vaccines, couldn't possibly be about spreading accurate medical information, but, instead, Dr. Malone has nothing better to do than be a misinformation spreader, and it's just unacceptable that he could possibly believe that the "approval process for the vaccines had been unwisely rushed", as the article quotes him saying. Let's keep in mind that these Covid vaccines were initiated by the United States government to "accelerate the development, manufacturing, and distribution of Covid-19 vaccines, therapeutics, and diagnostics" ("Operation Warp Speed" 2021). Nothing rushed there, right? So, isn't Dr. Malone entitled to have his opinion about how "unwisely rushed" these vaccines were, without being called a spreader of misinformation, or worse, a conspiracy theorist, which is basically anybody who has an opinion of their own? The amount of censorship about this is staggering, and clearly, like in the Atlantic article, there is a strong push to silence, or discredit anyone, especially doctors who could have their medical licenses suspended for sharing "misinformation" or "disinformation" about COVID-19 with their patients, according to a new California law, AB 2098 ("Doctors File First Lawsuit Challenging California Law That Seeks to Punish Physicians for COVID 'Misinformation'" 2022).

At this point, anything that goes against the mainstream media Covid narrative that keeps us obedient rule followers, is immediately categorized as misinformation, or conspiracy theories. This is getting old very quickly, and what is gaining great momentum is more people are waking up from the "mass formation" hypnosis that Dr. Mattias Desmet writes about in his book, *The Psychology of Totalitarianism*. I think after two years of being terrorized by threats that came from our government, the CDC, WHO, FDA, Anthony Fauci and the NIH, it's time for us to consciously un-crowd ourselves from the masses who went along with it, and that's exactly what the awakened are doing. They are going in the opposite direction of groupthink mentality, and choosing, consciously, not to be "sheeple", who are people that are compared to sheep in being docile, foolish, or easily led. For any of you sheeple who happen to be reading this book (bravo if you got this far), you can stop being led at any time, if you want to. Remember, it is a choice you have, so please ask yourself what are you gaining from being led, and if you are choosing to be led, where do you think you're being led to? Do you know, and can you explain it clearly in the same way "following the science" can be explained?

Those that are awake are open to hearing anything that makes sense. What they cannot do is un-awaken themselves to go along with any program, narrative, or complete nonsense that is being sold to be something other than complete nonsense. Please, let the duck theory be your mantra – "If it looks like a duck, swims like a duck, and quacks like a duck, then it probably is a duck." I know with certainty that the awakening has begun on a massive scale, and each day, I am completely inspired by how many more people I see who are waking up all over the world, and realizing that their freedom is far too important for it to be taken from them, and will do all that they can to protect it, fight for it, or even die for it; as many who are committed to waking up are willing to do. I'm not trying to pump this movement up as some kind of spiritual elitism, in the same way the global elites of the World Economic Forum are in co-hoots with billionaire elites all over the world, and think they're superior to us so they can mastermind our future. This isn't about, my movement is better than your movement, not that I think the global elites could care less about a spiritual movement. But, once they get wind of how strong and powerful this movement to awaken is, and threatening to their New World Order, global governance agenda, then maybe they will care, and who knows what they will do out of desperation to try and gain more power and control, which we will fight, every step of the way.

But the awakened will be ready, I can assure you. What I will say about this very powerful, soul burning movement to awaken, is this: It is why we are here, why we were born, and what we will remember, when we take our last breath. At that moment, when we depart this earth (which hopefully won't be inhabited by artificial intelligence), we will ask ourselves, "Was I awake? Was I brave? Was I unafraid to lead myself towards the truth that I believed in my heart was most real, when others told me differently?"

We know the answers already, don't we?

CHAPTER 24

Protect Our Children

We do not inherit the earth from our ancestors;
we borrow it from our children.

- CHIEF SEATTLE

Life is beautiful. Let the future generations cleanse
it of all evil, oppression, and violence, and enjoy it
to the full.

- LEON TROTSKY

The pandemic was extremely challenging for everyone, but no one has suffered more than our children. They had to experience a lockdown, which the name itself sounds frightening; school learning had to be done remotely, causing them to be on their computers for endless hours, which resulted in computer screen burn-out; they were isolated from their friends, and when they did return to school, they had to wear masks for long periods of time, many of them getting skin irritations and rashes, as well as many children complaining about difficulty in breathing, causing them deep anxiety, and depression. But, where it was most uncomfortable for them was the inability to see the faces of their teachers, friends, and anyone they came into contact with, making it impossible to read the expression on people's faces properly. Children, as we know, are most often responded to by adults with warm smiles, giving them a feeling of safety, comfort, and acceptance. And faces are one of the most important visual stimuli we perceive, which not only informs us about a person's identity, and things like sex and age, but also their mood, which was impossible for children to gauge. Imagine how difficult it must have been for them to listen to their teachers speak with their mouths covered by a mask, and not only have difficulty in understanding what they were saying, but also not being able to see their expressions while they were talking.

According to an article in USC Shaeffer, "Mandatory Masking of Children is a Bad Idea," it says "the bene-fits of masks in preventing serious illness or death from Covid-19 among children are infinitesimally small. At the same time, they are disruptive to learning and commu-nicating in classrooms. They may be partially effective in shielding adults from Covid, but since when is it ethical to burden children for the benefit of adults?" (Sood and

Bhattacharya 2021). And burdened they were, to the point where it bordered on cruelty, even child abuse, as many parents felt. The article goes on to say, "COVID-19 is less of a threat to children than accidents or the common flu. The survival rate among American children with confirmed cases is approximately 99.99%; remarkably, recent studies find an even higher survival rate."

This really makes you wonder why in the world would we have put children through such unnecessary stress and anxiety, to the point that we don't know the long term affects this will have on their mental health in the future. Suffice it to say, this has angered many parents who felt helpless as many of the LA and San Diego school districts (the largest in California) enforced these strict rules on their children that felt more like a punishment, and gave them worry that their parental rights were being taken from them to know what is best for their children. The LA and San Diego School Districts are being sued for their vaccine mandates, and the suits "contend that the vaccines have not been tested enough and that the mandates would subject unvaccinated students to discrimination and deprive them of their equal right to public education" (Spiegelman 2021). There were reported cases of isolating, shaming, and expelling children for not complying to the mask rules, even when the parents opposed their children having to wear them, especially if they had genuine health issues, like asthma, and no medical exemptions were allowed. To add insult to injury, when parents spoke to the schools about it at the school district meetings, pleading for their children to be spared the stress and anxiety they were experiencing, many of them felt they were not respected, and that some of the school board members were rude, and deliberately tuned them out. The term we heard on the news about parents being "domestic terrorists" because they were trying to protect their children, is unconscionable. According to an article, "AG Paxton Sues Biden Administration for Silencing Parents, Labeling Them 'Terrorists'" it says, "Attorney General Ken Paxton has joined Indiana in a Freedom of Information Act (FOIA) lawsuit to force the Biden Administration to release documents that will shed light on its labeling parents' domestic terrorists for voicing their opinions at school board meetings across the country".

In the article in USC Shaeffer, it goes on to say, "the long-term harm to kids from masking is potentially enormous. Masking is a psychological stressor for children and disrupts learning. Covering the lower half of the face of both teacher and pupil reduces the ability to communicate. In particular, children lose the experience of mimicking expressions, an essential tool of nonverbal communication. Positive emotions such as laughing and smiling become less recognizable, and negative emotions get amplified. Bonding between teachers and students takes a hit. Overall, it is likely that masking exacerbates the chances that a child will experience anxiety and depression, which are already at pandemic levels themselves" (Sood and Bhattacharya 2021). The authors of the article say that in their research they found that "in Sweden, where schools were not closed, and children were not masked, teachers were at lower Covid-19 risk than the rest of the population." In their opinion, they felt that "closing U.S. schools was a mistake as the harm to children likely exceeded the small benefit to adults."

But, unfortunately, it doesn't end there. The Covid-19 experimental shot controversy is a very hot topic concerning children. Being that "Covid-19 is less of a threat to children than accidents or the common flu", as the article stated, and "the survival rate among American children with confirmed cases is approximately 99.99%; remarkably, recent studies find an even higher survival rate"(Sood and Bhattacharya 2021), this has many parents fighting for their children not to be vaccinated with the Covid-19 experimental shot, not because they are anti-vaxxers, as they've been unfairly called, but because they don't trust it, or feel that it is safe, especially since it did not go through the proper clinical trials for children. It also has doctors like, Dr. Robert Malone, and Dr. Peter McCullough, vehemently speaking out against vaccinating children with the Covid-19 shot, especially children under 12, and pointing out the serious side-affects it can have on them like Myocarditis and Pericarditis, which are both related to inflammation of the heart muscle. In an article in Clark County, "'Health Nightmare': Dr. Robert Malone spotlights study on mRNA spike protein", Dr. McCullough said, "When the kids get myocarditis after the vaccine, 90% have to be hospitalized," McCullough said in a podcast interview in December. "They have dramatic EKG changes, chest pain, early heart failure, they need echocardiograms."

And, to make matters worse, there's a bill (SB866), which was trying to be passed by Senator Scott Weiner in California so that children as young as 12 years old can be vaccinated without parental consent, and means they can go to a pharmacy and get the Covid-19 shot without ever telling their parents, or if a clinic comes to their school, they can be pressured or coerced to get it, which would have been disastrous. It would be putting these young children in a horrible position to make major medical decisions for themselves that could potentially be dangerous, even life-threatening. Fortunately, that bill did not pass, even though Senator Weiner said, "This coalition isn't going anywhere" (Senator 2022). Once again, it is the "anti-vaxxers who are being blamed", as Weiner says, "The anti-vaxxers may have prevailed in this particular fight, but the broader fight for science and health continues." I would like Scott Weiner to be one of the people who can explain exactly what the science is when it comes to protecting children from this experimental vaccine. It makes you wonder what bill will be passed next that can harm millions of innocent children? A bill for them to be able to decide, also without parental consent, to begin hormone therapies, preparing them for gender transition surgery, which is a life altering decision they are not mature enough to make, and yet, they have to be 21 years old to buy alcohol?

These are very troubling times, dear reader, and especially for our children. If you believe in this Great Awakening, and subscribe to the idea that we are in the midst of a profound spiritual shift, our children will have a huge role in this evolution, which is why we need to do all that we can to protect them. The children who are living on this earth, and the ones who are being born, and will be born in the years to come, I believe, will possess the spiritual intelligence that we need to transform this planet. They are the pure light-beings, "starseeds"; who are special souls that are spiritually aware and will help raise the frequency of our consciousness. Think of how pure children's energy is, and if they are properly nurtured, fed, and guided, they will be our guides who will direct us with their bright light, to evolve our humanity as spiritual beings. It is crucial for those that are watching, teaching, or spending time with our children, that they are equipped to properly nurture them, and protect them from any harm or manipulation; mind, body and spirit. But sadly, their spirits have been tampered with, even hurt by the events that have happened to them during the pandemic, and we must help them recover and heal from the traumas they've experienced, unjustly.

Our children do not need anything to be put into their healthy bodies. They are strong, and resilient, and regarding the Covid-19 virus, again, they have a 99.99% survival rate ("recent studies find an even higher survival rate", as the article in USC Schaeffer mentioned), so why do we want to poison their perfect immune systems, with an experimental shot, when it is absolutely unnecessary? They are our adults of the future, so we must help them enter into adulthood, physically healthy and spiritually evolved to take on the challenges of things like trans-humanism, and artificial intelligence, and function with their natural traits and abilities that can transcend the limitations machines have. Transhumanists want you believing it is the other way around — that we will be the ones with the limitations, but our children will not, if we protect them at all costs from the evil forces that want to prey on them so they will not inherit this earth.

They will. The awakened ones will make sure that it happens, as it is meant to. There is no greater design than that of God's work, or the divine presence of natu-ral order, and children have a strong connection to what is most real, and divine, which is why when you observe them, they are so present and happy, as if they are in alignment with the sacred truths of the universe, naturally.

They are here on earth to transform this world into heaven on earth, salvaging the damage that adults have caused so mindlessly.

Conscious Evolution

Evolution of mankind is paralleled by the increase
and expansion of consciousness.

- ALBERT HOFMANN

Our evolution seems completely up for grabs, meaning there are people on this quickly changing planet who want to be in the driver's seat, controlling where the human race is going next. And there are many possibilities of where that can be, as I've spoken about. Some of those possibilities are: we could go in the direction of evolving beyond physical and mental limitations, by means of science and technology, as transhumanism offers us, or we can trust the people who feel that world governance would be optimum in directing our evolution; as those who subscribe to a New World Order believe, and we should just sit back and enjoy the ride.

The phrase, "Conscious evolution", was used early on by philosopher, social worker, and pioneer in the fields of organizational theory and behavior, Mary Parker Follett, in 1918. In her book, *The New State,* she writes about "seeing conscious evolution as the solution to society's problems of divisiveness and self-destruction brought on by our compulsive and shortsighted actions." And that is exactly what we are witnessing today, divisiveness and self-destruction being brought on by those who want to rule by control rather than letting us rule ourselves. Follett was considered the "mother of modern management", so I think she knew a thing or two about how people could work together more effectively. She believed, "rather than establishing a strict hierarchy and delegating power to certain individuals over others, leaders should practice co-active power". In the article "Mary Parker Follett – Creativity and Democracy", Nelson writes that Follett felt, "powering with your team is better than controlling them; this way, each member feels just as valued as the next". These are basic management theories Follett believed were most effective, but you can see how when not used on a fundamental level, powering over others can easily happen on a much larger scale, rather than "powering with people", as Follett said.

In the article, "The Management Theory of Mary Parker" (Peek 2018), Follett is quoted as saying, "leadership is not defined by the exercise of power but by the

capacity to increase the sense of power among those led."
Follett famously said, "The most essential work of the
leader is to create more leaders." I can see why Follett
was considered ahead of her time with such egalitarian
theories, especially being a woman telling male leaders
how to lead. Nelson writes in his article, "Mary Parker
Follett – Creativity and Democracy", "many contempo-
rary commentators hold that elements of Follett's work
have been integrated into mainstream thought and action
but never the full body of her vision and adaptive learning
framework. Peter Drucker said it was because it was too
radical for the times; Rosabeth Moss Kanter of Harvard
said it was too feminist for our male-dominated social
systems praxis; and Nitin Nohria of Harvard Business
School argued it was too utopian" (Nelson 2016). Too
utopian? We certainly could use some of Follett's utopian
theories, right about now, when we are slipping towards
what many are describing as a dystopia. I couldn't agree
with Nelson more, when he says, "Follett is such a powerful voice for today, especially when she said, 'Soft despotism is reinforced by our overly hierarchical conception
and reverence for expertise. It is a conception wherein we
turn over our power and authority to others in the belief
that they will always act in our interest. The rule of the
beneficent despot, the expert, and a muddled, befogged
people — our troubles will be over when we get enough
Intelligence Bureaus in Washington and enough scientific

expertise in our Universities, enough specialists in our
state and local governments ... then all life would become
fair and beautiful (Follett 1998). Such a mindset under-
mines citizenship because citizens are the final authority
in a democracy' (Follett, 1949)." Could there be more
accurate words to describe what we are dealing with right
now? For the last two years, we turned over our power
and authority to others in the belief that they will always
act in our interest, and they did not. We were misled
because we allowed the so-called experts and specialists
to tell us what to do, even when it went against our gut
instincts or higher intelligence. And what happened as
a result? "Soft despotism" was reinforced "by our overly
hierarchical conceptions and reverence for expertise," as
Follett said. When will we acknowledge that we need to
be led, and even have a greater need to be told what to
do? Do we not understand the wise words of Follett when
she says, "citizens are the final authority in a democracy"? How are we exercising our authority in a democracy
right now? We are not. We are giving our freedoms away,
one by one, and if we keep succumbing to these insidious
mandates, and extreme censorship, our freedoms will be
gone. If you don't see this happening, I'm afraid you are
not awake, and if you are awake, please spread this wide
and far! As author James Baldwin said so aptly, "Freedom
is not something that anybody can be given. Freedom is
something people take and people are free as they want to

be." I don't think you could say that about the doctors in California after Governor Newsom approved a bill that will "punish" doctors who spread "misinformation" about the prevention and treatments about Covid-19 (Myers 2022), and, as we know, spreading misinformation means going against the narrative to keep Covid-19, and the propaganda alive.

In order for us to achieve conscious evolution, we must stop believing that "our troubles will be over when we get enough Intelligence Bureaus in Washington and enough scientific expertise in our Universities, enough specialists in our state and local governments ... then all life would become fair and beautiful", as Follett said. Conscious evolution will not be realized if we are the "muddled, befogged people", which she called those who turn over their power, and we have, big time. I have repeatedly emphasized the urgent need to wake up at a time when, if we don't, we, the muddled, befogged people, will be led towards more censorship, more compliance, more despotic dominance, and control, and it will be too late to stop it. The global elites who are planning the New World Order, know exactly how muddled and befogged we are. They have planned, and systematically tested how awake or asleep we are, every step of the way, and we showed them how we were more asleep than awake, and that's exactly what they predicted about us. We passed all their tests with flying colors. We locked down, we masked, we distanced, we rolled up our sleeves eagerly (and continue to do with every booster they tell us to take), we ended friendships, we cut family members out of our life, we fired those who tirelessly served us at a time of need like our nurses did, we snitched on those who didn't comply, and made it very apparent we would do pretty much anything they asked us to do to stay alive. Are we really that predictable? How sad, or should I say pathetic that we can so easily give our power away because we desperately want to believe that "our troubles will be over, and "all life would become fair and beautiful", as Mary Parker Follett so perceptively believed.

How can conscious evolution possibly happen when you hear about things like World Economic Forum founder and boss, Klaus Schwab, not only talking about the New World Order of global governance, but also stating that "by 2030 he wants microchips implanted inside all human bodies, and predicts that Big Tech firms will increasingly pursue implanted microchips and other transhumanist technologies" (Pie 2021). For anyone who is reading this book, and not familiar with Klaus Schwab, and his brain-reading technology plan for our future, get to know everything you can about him, so that you will be very aware of the type of totalitarianism, and transhumanism ideas he has in store for our evolution. You might also like to know, as I discovered in my deep dive what these power-hungry people are up to, that his fellow transhumanist, Mark Zuckerberg, (creator of the new and improved virtual reality, Metaverse), is busy working on a robot "butler" named Jarvis, "to control his home iron man style" (Wagner 2016). The thought of millions of people still asleep, and completely unaware of agendas like this for our future, truly amazes me. I would love nothing more to not have someone like Klaus Schwab in the foreground of my mind, or read about Mark Zuckerberg's human-enhancement fantasies, but when you awaken, and want to know what's going on, and I mean really going on, unfortunately, you become aware of people like them, and it is very disturbing, to say the least. The good news is that there are also millions of people all over the world who are aware of this, and they are diligently working in all sorts of ways to make sure that the dystopian visions of people like Klaus Schwab, or anyone who is trying to put us on a fast track towards artificial intelligence hell, doesn't force itself on us, against our will.

I'm not saying that all these science-fiction type of ideas for the future are intended to be bad, or do us harm, especially if it can help someone with a disability to use a smartphone with their mind, if they can't use their hands, but still, a brain chip seems that it can go terribly wrong, if we're not careful. By the way, someone asked me if I knew what "smart" means, when we call our mobile phone a "smartphone", and I did not. They informed me that there is an acronym for smart (don't even bother finding this on the internet), and it is: S = "Surveillance", M = "Monitoring", A = "Access", R = "Rating", and T = "Tracking". Is this a conspiracy theory? I guess time will tell.

Even someone like Elon Musk, has repeatedly warned that "Artificial Intelligence will soon become just as smart as humans", and said that when it does "we should all be scared because humanity's very existence is at stake" (Shead 2020). What he is referring to is DeepMind, "which is a research lab acquired by Google in 2014 for a reported $600 million, and best known for developing AI systems that can play games better than any human." The article also says, Musk, who profited from an early investment in DeepMind, told The New York Times that "his experience of working with AI at Tesla means he is able to say with confidence that we're headed toward a situation where AI is vastly smarter than humans." But the most troubling thing he said was that "he believes the time frame is less than five years. That doesn't mean everything goes to hell in five years. It just means that things get unstable or weird" (Shead 2020).

And that's what so many of us are feeling, already — that things are getting very unstable and weird, and for a lot of people, they don't know why they have an unsettling feeling, or experiencing anxiety or depression. I've spoken to people who have not felt like themselves for the last few years, and they don't even know why. I've asked

myself; how can they possibly not know what's going on?
Maybe if they did, they would understand why they feel
the way they do, and who wouldn't feel off, or troubled
by so many things I'm bringing up in this book. I would
love nothing more than to just keep this about Mindfulness, and tell you how good you can feel if you practice
being present with total awareness, which you can. But
Mindfulness makes you extremely aware of what you are
seeing, and based on everything that's going on today, you
are going to see an awful lot, and not all of it is going to
be pleasant or reassuring as far as where our humanity is
headed. But it will also help you appreciate what is good
that exists in the world too. We mustn't let what we see
that is weighing heavily on our hearts, rob us of the lovely,
and meaningful things in life too. There is so much natural beauty all around us, it is truly mind-boggling why the
transhumanists want to play God, and tamper with divine
law.

Join me, dear reader, in bringing forward a conscious
(r)evolution. You, me, and the collective consciousness on
the planet, as well as Anima Mundi, the world soul, are all
working together to birth Our New World. Things may
be unstable or weird right now, but if we stay on track,
what awaits us, will be magnificent and wondrous.

"We carry a new world here, in our hearts. That world is growing this minute."

- Buenaventura Durruti

CHAPTER 26

The Future Is Here

I never think of the future - it comes soon enough.

- ALBERT EINSTEIN

No one saves us but ourselves. No one can and no
one may. We ourselves must walk the path.

- GAUTAMA BUDDHA

I spoke about this being a time of a Great Awakening, and
throughout history, there have been other Great Awakenings that occurred, causing people to search for deeper
meaning in their lives, and for many of those people, religion
was not the answer, which is why it was waning. Most of
the past Great Awakenings were thought of as religious
revivals because of the lack of enthusiasm for religion, but

something different is going on with our Great Awakening that no other time can be compared to it. With churches, temples, and mosques closed during the pandemic, because they were not considered "essential", (but, as I mentioned, liquor stores remained open the entire time), we now face the possibility of always being at the effect of the World Health Organization declaring "states of emergency", whenever a virus comes down the pike, therefore making places of worship not where people can seek refuge. That means we must rely on ourselves to "walk the path", as Buddha spoke of, and will have to save ourselves because "no one can and no one may", as Buddha also said. Welcome to the future, dear reader, for we are living at a time when we must save ourselves from the future that has arrived "soon enough", as Einstein said, and it is a future we never could have imagined being quite like this.

Where will you go, and what will you do when the things that have kept us feeling safe and secure, no longer will, and relying on things like the government, political leaders, health organizations, and the pharmaceutical industry to keep us medicated for our ills that have mostly been caused by the stresses those controlling systems have caused, prove to be detrimental to our wellbeing, and we now must be the ones who step up to not only save ourselves, but our entire humanity, and this planet we are occupying. What type of promising future ahead do we think awaits us when we find ourselves in a well-planned future of today, that was being masterminded by people in power we believed in, voted for, gave our money to, and even fought others defending, that were setting us up all along for putting our humanity at serious risk, like it is right now.

Yes, our future, which has been strategically planned, and funded to be "pandemic simulated", by people like Bill Gates, has arrived, and the reason it looks as "weird" and "unstable", as Elon Musk said things would get, is probably because of our deliberate unconsciousness to not want to know the truth, and keep ourselves in a type of hypnotic denial. And now we find ourselves facing a type of ongoing future that Klaus Schwab, and the global elites have masterminded for us, and if we don't acknowledge-where our very uncertain future is headed, it will likely have us being forced to get vaccinated against our will, with no end in sight, because they (those who can decide our fate for us because they feel they are entitled to play God), keep moving the goal post every time another virus comes along (we've been living with viruses since the beginning of time so why all of a sudden are we needing to be vaccinated with every single new variant this pandemic has caused?) We will have no medical freedom, no longer able to eat meat because the Impossible Burger will be the new "fake" meat, and according to Organic Consumers Association, "Emperor Gates has a new decree: All rich countries should move to 100% synthetic beef" (Purdy

2017). Have you not wondered why is Gates investing in everything that pertains to our lives (and our survival), like vaccines, food, and now farmland? I recommend reading a very eye-opening article in Regeneration International, "Vandana Shiva: Bill Gates Empires Must Be Dismantled" (Dr Joseph Mercola 2021).

The CEO of Impossible Foods, Patrick Brown says, "his genetically engineered synthetic meat substitutes will replace the use of animals by 2035" ("Reject Bill Gates' Impossible Burger" 2022). I happen to be a vegetarian, but what I'd like to ask you meat eaters out there, is this the "meatless" future you imagined for yourself? But wait, it gets more horrifying. The Food and Agriculture Organization is anticipating scarcities of agriculture land, "Bill Gates has amassed nearly 270,000 acres of farmland across the country, making him the largest farmland owner in America" (Marcelo 2022). I'm sure he'll be buying a lot more while we're eating our "meatless burger that bleeds", but do not despair, the Food and Agriculture Organization feels that there's a solution in store for us other than eating synthetic meat substitutes, and that solution is insects! "Eating insects is as old as mankind", an article in The Conversation, says, and we really should consider that, "insects are rich in nutrients such as amino acids", which, by the way "are often absent in conventional food" (Niassy and Ekesi 2017). Who knew!

So, what should we expect next, as we slip into this

dystopian future that we find ourselves already getting familiar with because the global elites are dropping hints that it's coming in full force? It's starting to feel like we're in the Metaverse, but just don't know it. You can see how these very "weird" and "unstable" times can have you thinking all sorts of things, and as a friend of mine said recently, "I just don't know what to believe anymore." If crazy is our "new normal" then what kind of ongoing future will the new-crazy-normal be? Will we just continue to out-crazy ourselves into oblivion? No, we mustn't allow for that, but the only way for it not to happen is if the awakened ones get into the driver's seat of this fast-moving starship, and "restore freedom and justice to the Galaxy", as was done in the Star Wars movie, *A New Hope*. We seem to be functioning under the dark orders similar to that of "cruel Darth Vader" in Star Wars, only we have more than one evil "Dark Father" telling us what to do. There are many dark players planning this future agenda for us, as I have mentioned, and if we don't act quickly, they will control this galaxy exactly as they want to, which at this point, they already seem to be doing.

We may be in the grips of a future we never anticipated, but that doesn't mean we can't shift its direction to save our freedom, as more and more people awaken, and they are, all over the world. Dear reader, I trust that you are one of the many freedom fighters who has joined this history making movement to fight and resist a New

World Order, and lead us towards Our New World, where we will be free to decide what that will be. But, again, the only way, and I do mean only way that can happen is if more people awaken, for we need to be the majority that occupies the human race on the planet. The future is here, and it has arrived as one of the greatest spiritual shifts we have ever seen in our lifetime. This is what we have been getting ready for, and you, dear reader, are a very important part of this shift. If you have chosen the path of awakening, then you are someone who is helping to lead us to Our New World, and will have people like us living as awakened souls, which is the purpose of our life on earth. We are not meant to be asleep, or led towards a world that is designed to annihilate our soul so that artificial intelligence can take our place, and we no longer will be conscious enough to even know it. Remember, Elon Musk said that AI is humanity's "biggest existential threat", and even physicist, Stephen Hawking said, "The development of full artificial intelligence could spell the end of the human race."

Our job, to stop a New World "Order" (an authoritative command) takeover, is to develop ourselves as fully, conscious human beings, and let us be the super humans (not computers) of today, and the future of tomorrow.

CHAPTER 27

How To Keep Consciousness Alive

I think we have a duty to maintain the light of consciousness to make sure it continues into the future.

- ELON MUSK

According to an article in Scientific American, "Today's Biggest Threat: The Polarized Mind", one of the major threats to humanity is a mind that is "fixated on a single point of view to the utter exclusion of competing points of view", and if one possesses a polarized mind, "consciousness cannot flourish until it counterbalances and, to the extent possible, supersedes the polarized mind."

The authors, Kirk J. Schneider and Sayed Mohsen Fatemi, both psychologists, say that they "have arrived at the conclusion that so much of what we call human de-

pravity ("evil") seems to be based on the polarized mind",
so how do we connect their astute findings to a time
when censorship and cancel-culture are part of this "new
normal" we find ourselves in, and the polarized mind
doesn't appear to be making room for any "competing
points of view", which makes it impossible for consciousness to "flourish."

The article says that there are many factors that contribute to the polarized mind, but two of the "common
denominators" among all of them appears to be fear and
anxiety, and that is when people tend to become polarized, and "fixated and extreme – in the face of helplessness, anxiety and fear." As I've spoken about, fear and
anxiety were what most people were feeling during the
pandemic, and an overwhelming feeling of helplessness
permeated the globe. What we found ourselves dealing
with was the highest level of polarization we've ever seen,
and never before have more people been divided over
their respective beliefs about the pandemic. And, if you
didn't go along with the narrative that the government
or health officials jammed down our throats all day, every
day, it just increased the polarization, and this "human depravity" — this "evil" that the authors speak about, is what
has been overpowering us, to the point that our humanity
has never felt as threatened as it does right now.

People have felt that their lives are at stake with the
Covid-19 virus, but that is mostly because they are being

told this incessantly, so how can they overcome their fear of "death anxiety", if all they hear is that they should be afraid of the next variant that's coming, so, basically, we are being kept hostage to living life in a perpetual state of fear of dying. I've gone over that, and explained that unless you overcome your personal fears, you will pretty much be at the mercy of everything that makes you feel that your survival is in danger, and live life in a heightened state of fear all of the time, which is completely unnatural, and exceedingly stressful. The article goes on to say that the polarized mind "not only tends to make people feel small and insignificant, but ultimately – if the helplessness, anxiety and fear are strong enough, people will do all they can to avoid such death anxiety, including becoming violent and oppressive themselves as a defense" (Fatemi and Schneider 2019).

Can we not see how we are living like rats in a cage being experimented on? We are being fed fear daily, and it is having detrimental effects on us, psychologically and physically, and causing us to behave in all sorts of unnatural, and potentially dangerous ways. How in the world can our consciousness flourish if we can't even get out of our own "polarized mind's" way, by not allowing for a single "competing point of view" to permeate our fixed beliefs, that have us functioning like despots who are acting irrationally, even cruelly towards one another.

What have we allowed ourselves to become? And who

have we allowed to provoke us to become this way? We must ask ourselves these questions before it is too late. This human depravity – this evil that these psychologists speak about is very real, and we need to acknowledge that our humanity is being seriously threatened, and if we don't do something about it, I fear what's to come, and that is a genuine fear to have. But we can resist this evil, and that is why awakening is absolutely critical. The only way for consciousness to "continue into the future", as Elon Musk says in his quote, is for us to make sure that it does, and it can, if we become more actively aware of how our consciousness (awareness of ourselves, others, and the world), must be protected from all the harm that is coming at it. Those that are in control and want to determine our future by bringing in a New World Order, want nothing more than for us not to be conscious and aware of what they are really doing, which is why questioning their agenda is so threatening to them, and they hold the deprecating label of conspiracy theory over our heads like an authoritarian banner. Think of them as anti-consciousness. Our awakening is anathema to them. And, if a vision for our future is one of soullessness, which the transhumanists, and global elites seem to want for us, then we will become the super computers they would like us to be, and that means an end to human consciousness, as we know it. Our awareness of ourselves will be gone, and we will no longer perceive the world through a filter of human emotional intelligence where we can properly gauge our behaviors and actions. We have already seen what a pandemic can do to us, and when we are told to be in fear 24/7, and believe that our survival is threatened, human beings can turn on others who don't agree with their polarized mind, which we saw many people do. Fear can bring out a fierce animal nature in people, causing them to behave like savages. It reminds me of the book, *Lord of the Flies*, which explored the dark side of humanity, and the savagery that can happen to the most civilized human beings. The author, William Golding, brilliantly explores "humankind's intrinsic evil nature", and I remember when I read it as a young woman, I found it very disturbing.

If we allow ourselves to be polarized, we will not succeed at overcoming this human depravity – this evil that seems to have taken hold of many people's minds. You must believe me when I say that the powers that be, those people in positions of authority who you may have put your trust and faith in the last few years when you were scared and vulnerable, are the very ones who stoked the fire of fear, causing us to be so polarized from one another, that many people, out of fear, went so far as to cut precious loved ones out of their life, and for some grandparents, their own children forbid them to see their grandchildren, if they weren't vaccinated. Do you not see how they turned family members against one another?

We must remember that the president of the United
States, Joe Biden, also stoked the fear, and abandoned the
constitution by "Declaring War against Unvaccinated"
(Duey Stroebel State Senator 2021). The unvaccinated
were singled out, like some kind of witch hunt, and were
threatened because of their medical choices. If our own
president can declare a war against the unvaccinated, you
can see, as clear as day, how we were set up to have our
mind's fertile with polarizing poison, in an extremely
dangerous way.

How convenient is it for history to be erased from
our minds, and at the rate that censorship and cancel
culture are going, before we know it, something like the
Holocaust will be wiped clean from our history books,
and our children will never know how preying on the fear
and vulnerabilities of people is exactly how Hitler rose
to power. We must be consciously aware of our ability to
have a fixed, or polarized mind, and if we don't, we can
easily slip into this human depravity, and that is when evil
seeps into our minds, and destroys our ability to "maintain
the light of consciousness", that Elon Musk speaks of.

I thought it was interesting that the authors of the
article mentioned that mindlessness is "a condition of
narrowed perception and reactivity", and I was happy to
see that they mentioned Mindfulness, which is having a
mental state of heightened awareness, as "a cardinal feature of the depolarized mind." The only way we can keep

consciousness alive and maintain the light of it to "continue into the future", as Elon Musk said, is for us to practice Mindfulness diligently, and keep ourselves in a state of "Illumined Mind", which means, a mind no longer of higher thought, but of spiritual light.

So, how can we keep our mind illumined with spiritual light? We must have a self-reflective mindset, and observe our thoughts, feelings, behaviors and actions, and question them, and our intentions.

If one is not willing to reflect and observe themselves with total awareness, or feel they are above needing to evaluate their opinions, behaviors, and actions, to see if they are correct or reasonable, they are likely to be the ones who don't question themselves at all, and egotistically feel that everything they think and do, is extremely important, or superior to what others think and do, and keeps them in a fixed mind-set, which is the very thing that creates the polarized mind. There is no room for spiritual light in a polarized mind, and those who possess one are more likely to stop at nothing for their fixed views to dominate others.

Isn't that what we're witnessing with people like Bill Gates, Mark Zuckerberg, Klaus Schwab, and those that want to control and dominate others? This also includes the institutions and private companies that own Twitter (we will see what Elon Musk does with it), and mainstream media that controls all "competing points of view".

I see no signs of spiritual light coming from those elites, who are the wealthiest, and most powerful people in the world. It seems all they want to do is dominate the entire globe, and not allow for any (competing) points of view, whatsoever, to get in the way of their fixed, New World Order views. I have no doubt that people like that are the ones creating the human depravity – the very evil that we are feeling is upon us, which again, is why awakening is what we absolutely must do, individually, and collectively.

To win this spiritual war, we must not only maintain our light of consciousness, but usher in a type of light that will blind those who wish to destroy it.

CHAPTER 28

The Day
The World Woke Up

The universe grows smaller every day, and the
threat of aggression by any group, anywhere, can
no longer be tolerated. There must be security for
all, or no one is secure. Now, this does not mean
giving up any freedom, except the freedom to act
irresponsibly.

- KLAATU

For anyone who's never seen the sci-fi thriller, *The Day The Earth Stood Still* (the original movie was directed by Robert Wise in 1951, the remake directed by Scott Derrickson in 2008), it's thought of as a classic with a prophetic message. The synopsis, in a nutshell, is a humanoid alien comes to earth, and demands that its leaders choose between peace or destruction. Both films "touch on timeless, mythic themes like destruction and redemption, death and resurrection, mortality and immortality, individual liberty and group unity, national sovereignty and global community, and, of course, scientists playing God and technology run amok" (Shermer 2008). I would say that's a pretty good description of what's going on right now, but instead of focusing on an alien demanding that we cool it on the destruction of our planet, I'd like to spin the title and focus on "The Day The World Wakes Up", to finally do something about us destroying ourselves.

We've gotten plenty of warnings about how we are destroying the planet, and maybe it hasn't come from an alien (yet), but we certainly have been hearing about how we are polluting the earth by burning fossil fuels, causing climate change, dumping waste into our oceans, ongoing deforestation, and to add to that, violence increasing exponentially. I feel that I've been hearing warnings about the destruction of our planet for as long as I can remember, but as I look back at my life, and my children's lives, I think of what kinds of solutions do I remember hearing about, or being taught in school how we can help clean up the environment and save our planet, and I don't recall anything significant, or life changing, other than recycling, or doing away with plastic straws and bags, and occasionally cleaning up the beaches. The first event to raise awareness on a large scale was when we celebrated Earth

Day on April 22nd, 1970. I remember being excited because it was the day before my birthday, and I thought it was neat that it would make it even more meaningful.

Earth Day made it clear that Americans understood, and were very concerned about the deterioration of our environment, and also raised awareness all over the globe, and continues to do so with each Earth Day anniversary. According to Cision PR Newswire, "The 50th Anniversary Of Earth Day Unites Tens Of Millions of People Across The World In Action And A Multi- Platform Event", it says, "despite 3.9 billion people sheltering in place and the tragedy of the pandemic, over 100 million people took action in 192 countries in honor of Earth Day's 50th Anniversary. Mayors, national governments, and multilaterals made commitments on a wide range of environmental issues, including climate literacy, plastics, renewable energy, and other issues, while faith groups around the world held virtual prayer services in support of ending climate change. People pledged to vote, parents and teachers educated millions of their students and children about climate change and environmental issues, and hundreds of millions of trees were planted" (Network 2020). That all sounds very pro-active, but I don't recall much being said about the recent Earth Day Anniversary, and it seems to me that most people were still pre-occupied with getting Covid, and not one person I was around expressed a concern about the environment, but was more upset about how they might be forced to take one more booster, or that their children would have to return back to school, and forced to wear a mask, yet again, even after the CDC, and Fauci expressed it does not prevent you from getting Covid.

Earth Day lasts 24 hours, and as much as I think it's nice that faith groups around the world held virtual prayer services in support of ending climate change, and people pledged to vote, why do we find ourselves 71 years after the first version of The Day The Earth Stood Still was released, still grappling with the same themes about destruction we did back then? Has anything really changed, because it seems to me that we're still talking about the same problems, and still worried that we're going to destroy ourselves and the planet, and we most certainly could, but it won't be just because of something like climate change, I can assure you. Even now, with what's happening in the Netherlands, and the farmers having their farmland taken from them unless they reduce their use of nitrogen, it's hard to trust that this is really (just) about protecting the environment, and could it be that governments are trying to control everything (New World Order), including farmers and their farmland (remember, Bill Gates is buying up an inordinate amount of farmland in North America, with no end in sight, and he's part of the New World Order, global governance agenda). According to an article, "Netherlands: The

Summer Of Discontent", it says, "the Netherlands has descended into an ideological war zone between city-bound bureaucrats trying to polish their climate credentials on the world stage, and local farmers who have been feeding Europe for centuries." As one farmer said, "This is not a democracy anymore: it's a dictatorship."

So, what's really going on, and by that, I mean, what's going on all over the world? There seems to be a connect-the-dots series of events that are popping up all over the world, and are we just to assume that it's because of climate change concerns? I don't think so. Dr. Robert Malone, in his newsletter, mentions the "World Economic Forum 2030 agenda and the farmer protests regarding having their farmlands taken from them, together with other forced draconian measures." He also says, "there is a huge movement within the Netherlands by main stream media to suppress information about these measures and the protests from reaching the people, and because of the information suppression, because of the EU involvement – the government will win this fight" ("Robert W Malone MD," n.d.). And, it does look like many governments are aiming to win the fight to control people by censoring or cancelling them, even freezing their bank accounts as Prime Minister Justin Trudeau did to the truckers who were protesting draconian measures to get vaccinated against their will, and denied their right to choose bodily autonomy (Loh 2022). And now we're seeing in other

parts of the world, farmers having their farmland taken
from them if they don't comply, including Amish organic
farmers – ("Amish Farmer Faces Fines, Prison Time for
Refusing to Comply with USDA Regulations, FEE –
Foundation for Economic Education"), so what's next?
Well, as I've said, unless we wake up, and take our power
back, I suspect more farmland will be taken, more control
over people will occur at a rapid speed, which means more
of our civil liberties and freedoms will be lost, all in the
name of what, "Agenda 2030"? This agenda is supposedly
about "Sustainable Development Goals or Global Goals"
("United Nations Development Programme (UNDP)"
n.d.), and "are a collection of 17 interlinked global goals
designed to be a 'blueprint to achieve a better and more
sustainable future for all.' These goals, also called "SDGs",
were "set up in 2015 by the United Nations General
Assembly and are intended to be achieved by 2030." So,
let me ask you this. If this agenda is really about a "more
sustainable future for all", what's with all the censorship,
and cancel-culture? There's something about truly caring
about us and our future that doesn't coincide with taking
away our first amendment – freedom of speech (which
is the cornerstone of our democracy), and being forced,
against our will, to go along with medical mandates
without conformed consent, and other threats of our civil
liberties, and constitutional rights. Has there suddenly
become a new hybrid objective, which consists of "global

goals" and tyranny? We really need to pay very close attention to the very clever wording of so called "sustainable development goals", and what we're consenting to.

Could it be that the climate crisis, or as Al Gore referred to it in his 2006 documentary, *An Inconvenient Truth,* which emphasized a need to "act immediately to reduce greenhouse gas emissions" ("SuperSummary" n.d.), has been the number one focal point of our greatest concern for the future, all the while, other things (or should I say agendas) were being ushered in, unbeknownst to us, that should now be our deepest concerns about a greater threat to our freedom and sovereignty. Yes, it's extremely important to care about the environment, but not if that means we're going to be enslaved while the United Nations, along with the World Economic Forum, and the global elites, decide what our SDGs should be. And let's not forget that these same global elites are known to fly their private jets to the climate conferences in Davos. Please connect the dots, dear reader!

Let's try and remain optimistic, despite the alarming changes we're seeing (for those that are awake enough to see them), and pray that others will wake up, hopefully sooner than later. Perhaps we should gather together in faith groups around the world and hold virtual prayer the way people did on the 50th Earth Day Anniversary, and pray that this global awakening will happen as soon as possible. Prayer can be very powerful, but you need to get a lot more people on board to pray for the world to wake up, and that's extremely challenging when so many people are still asleep. They are clueless about what's really going on and prefer letting people in positions of power make decisions for them, which is proving to be very dangerous for all of us.

Please make your own decisions and decide for yourself what you need to do to hold onto your freedoms, no matter what. Be bold, dear reader, and stand up for what you believe. If each and every one of us was being the change that Gandhi told us to be, we would see the changes we wish for. Are you ready for that? I know I am. Now let's go out into the world and emanate the light and truth as much as we possibly can, and get others on board to do it with us.

"Goodness is a bright flame within you. Use it to light up the world."

— Frank Sonnenberg

CHAPTER 29

Who Will Lead The Way?

Do not follow where the path may lead. Go instead where there is no path and leave a trail.

- RALPH WALDO EMERSON

If I were to ask you if you believe that Jesus was either a God, man, or myth, what would you say? I can't know your answer, but I can tell you mine, which is I can't know for sure if Jesus existed because I can only go by what has been written in biblical texts, so therefore, he could be God, man, or completely made up as part of a grand historical narrative.

For religious Christians, Jesus is their savior, and they believe in the Second Coming, which according to biblical prophecy, "The righteous dead will be resurrected, and together with the righteous living, they will be glorified and taken to heaven, and the unrighteous will die." For religious Jews, they believe in the first coming, and that the long-awaited Messiah, who is not Jesus Christ, but a future Jewish king who has been anointed, will deliver Israel from all oppressors and lead them into a golden age.

Could it be that the reason most people want to be led, other than not having to make decisions for themselves, is that they want to believe there's someone they can trust who will lead them into some type of "golden age", or at least, peace of mind during a pandemic, and if that person is deemed an authority figure, it's easy to project onto them savior qualities. That explains why someone like Anthony Fauci was regarded as some kind of "lord", as he was jokingly called at one point, and someone even played on that by writing a book called, *All Hail Lord Fauci: King of Kings, Lord of Masks, Keeper of the Seven Sacred Sacraments: For New Believers in the Church of Covid. Your Covid-19 Political Joke Gift Paperback by James Jordon* (yes, that is really the title). Clearly, it was some kind of joke to write a book with that name, but the author even went as far as to write their own ten commandments, the first one being, "Thou shalt always weareth thy mask. If possible, weareth two masks, but never less than one mask shall thou weareth", and the tenth commandment, "Thou shall never question approved authority". That commandment actually strikes a very familiar chord for those who know by now that's exactly what propagated the conspiracy theory label — questioning authority. Author James Jordon seems to have a type of humor that might be considered either way over the top, or spot on to what he's poking fun of, and to add to the point he was trying to make, he begins the book with his re-worded quote from Revelation 6:8, "And I looked, and behold a pale horse: and his name that sat on him was Death, and Hell followed with him. And power was given unto them over the fourth part of the earth, to kill…with hunger, and with pestilence."

Oh, dear reader, what a time this is! How can we possibly believe we're going to be led into some type of golden age when what we've been hearing of late is that we're headed towards a New World Order, and this new world will be designed from a "blueprint to achieve a better and more sustainable future for all" (Ellerbeck 2022). And, to assure us that it's going to be everything we could possibly want, we will "own nothing, have no privacy, and life will never be better" (Auken 2016). I was quite taken aback to see that this article was written in November, 2016, and if it doesn't get you thinking how in the world could Ms. Auken, who was the first Danish politician to be a young global leader for the World Economic Forum, have written something like this without everything we're seeing now play out on the world stage, hasn't been planned ahead very strategically. This is what she writes:

"Once in a while I get annoyed about the fact that I

have no real privacy. Nowhere I can go and not be registered. I know that, somewhere, everything I do, think and dream of is recorded. I just hope that nobody will use it against me. All in all, it is a good life. Much better than the path we were on, where it became so clear that we could not continue with the same model of growth. We had all these terrible things happening: lifestyle diseases, climate change, the refugee crisis, environmental degradation, completely congested cities, water pollution, air pollution, social unrest and unemployment. We lost way too many people before we realized that we could do things differently" (Auken 2016).

And, if that doesn't have you shaking your head in total disbelief, how about when Ms. Auken writes this:

"Shopping? I can't really remember what that is. For most of us, it has been turned into choosing things to use. Sometimes I find this fun, and sometimes I just want the algorithm to do it for me. It knows my taste better than I do by now."

How easy would it be for me to say, "okay, everyone, just let 'the algorithm' do it for you because it knows our taste better than we do by now", but I can't. As much as this makes me want to weep for future generations, I know I must remain strong, and steadfast in believing that if we give into this horrific, dystopian agenda that's been planned for us all along, then you know who will lead the way? Artificial intelligence will lead every step of the way in the not too distant future, which has already "come soon enough", as Einstein said.

Here is a chilling quote I want to share with you that drives home how we cannot stand idly by:

"He was oppressed, and he was afflicted, yet he opened not his mouth: he is brought as a lamb to the slaughter, and as a sheep before her shearers is dumb, so he openeth not his mouth."

— Isaiah 53:7

"Like sheep to the slaughter", is a phrase which refers to the theory that Jews went passively to their deaths during the Holocaust. Abba Kovner, a Polish Israeli poet, writer, and partisan leader, who tried to organize an uprising in the Vino Ghetto in Lithuania, along with other Jewish resistance leaders, used the phrase to strongly encourage Jews to fight back ("Abba Kovner," n.d.). Apparently, in postwar Israel, there were some who demonized Holocaust survivors as having gone like sheep to the slaughter, which implied they were partly responsible for their own suffering and death because they didn't resist, which towards the end of their lives, was far too late for them to fight back. My father lost his entire family in the Holocaust, and so many times I asked myself how could this type of unimaginable evil ever have happened?

I will always wonder if the Jews could have tried to save their lives much sooner, but tragically, they waited far too long, as if they couldn't believe that this type of evil could possibly exist, and enough of them did not "openeth" their mouths when perhaps they could have. Is that what we're doing? Keeping our mouths shut when we should be talking about how we have "no real privacy" as Ida Auken wrote in her article back in 2016, and there's nowhere we can go and "not be registered", and that somewhere, everything we "do, think and dream of is recorded", and can only "hope that nobody will use it against us".

Is this what we are going to allow to happen:

"Welcome to the year 2030. Welcome to my city - or should I say, 'our city.' I don't own anything. I don't own a car. I don't own a house. I don't own any appliances or any clothes."

Would you be happy?

Wake up, for God's sake! Wake up!

CHAPTER 30

Realistic Utopianism

A map of the world that does not include Utopia is not worth even glancing at, for it leaves out the one country at which Humanity is always landing. And when Humanity lands there, it looks out, and seeing a better country, sets sail. Progress is the realization of Utopias.

- OSCAR WILDE

We want our Utopia now.

- SINCLAIR LEWIS

One of the definitions of utopianism is "the belief or pursuit of a state in which everything is perfect, typically regarded as unrealistic or idealistic" ("Utopia - New World Encyclopedia," n.d.).

In Thomas More's book, *Utopia,* he described a society that was significantly better than England as it existed at the time, so is it unrealistic to think or dream about a society, or world that could be better than the one we are experiencing presently? It seems that someone like Mark Zuckerberg, who has created what he thinks is a better world in his Metaverse, finds it very realistic to share it with as many people as he possibly can so they can feel exactly as he does, and since he was able to manifest what the Economic Times says "represents a nirvana for technophiles" (The Economic Times, 2022), I imagine that his vision wasn't called "unrealistic" or "idealistic", because when you're a billionaire, or a global elite, people probably don't question or challenge your ideas, and are readily accepted by other like-minded, elite people.

Being that we are living in a time that is starting to appear more dystopian by the minute, especially when you hear things like, "by 2030, you will own nothing, have no privacy, and life will never be better" (Auken 2016), I think Sinclair Lewis' quote, "We want our Utopia now", is exactly how we should feel, and our utopia will not be a world where we will own nothing, and have no privacy. No, our utopia will be a much better world because we will have survived the lunacy of these people like Zuckerberg, Bill Gates, Klaus Schwab, and whoever else is part of this New World Order that's threatening our humanity by forcing us to live out their dystopian fantasies, and pretending that it will be a better world, which we know damn well it won't be.

The world they want for us is anything but utopian, but they will have you believing otherwise, if you're not careful, which is why being awake is the most important thing you can do in your life right now. Dear reader, I know you're smart enough to see right through these kinds of absurd lies, but did you ever ask yourself why those who created this dystopian vision, this "blueprint to achieve a better and more sustainable future for all" (United Nations 2015), which includes eating fake meat, and crickets, believed that people like us would be stupid enough to buy into this, and sadly, many people were, and still are. Even now, when you talk to people who bought into the Covid experimental vaccine narrative, and took as many as four shots (and probably would take more if they were told to), even after they got Covid, which our government and health officials assured us the vaccines would prevent us from getting Covid and transmitting it, those poor souls are still holding onto this bogus narrative with all of their might. I've seen some of them look down when asked about taking the vaccine, as if they are embarrassed to admit that maybe, just maybe, they bought into a program that is now completely imploding, and yet, they will still say what I have heard repeated by many, as if it's a rote response; "well, I would have gotten much sicker, or even died, if I hadn't been vaccinated." That is a lie. There are millions of people who got vaccinated and got Covid badly, and even died, but what else can these people say. "I was lied to, and stupid enough to believe it?"

We must stop this dystopian circus and demand our utopia now. We needn't give into one more minute of this nightmare by going along with it, and that means being fed up enough to stop giving into what you're being told to do by those you deem as authority figures, who claim they know what is better for you. They are the ones who are designing goals for us, and deceptively call it a "blueprint to achieve a better and more sustainable future for all." Really? A better future is not owning nothing, having no privacy, and eating fake meat and crickets. That is hell, and if you don't see it for what it is, a feudalistic vision, you will live out their dystopian reality for them like a peasant. A better future is one that is designed by us, and intended to live, not only sustainably, but having the freedom to self-govern, which these tyrannical elites do not want for us. They want us to be completely dependent on them, which is why they are trying, so desperately, to implement global governance.

We know what is good for us, just like an animal knows who is good, and doesn't want to hurt them. They also know who does, and sense it immediately. I don't feel that any of the people I have mentioned throughout this book, like Anthony Fauci, Bill Gates, Mark Zuckerberg, Klaus Schwab, and anyone else who wants to control us, truly cares about our well-being, because if they did, their New World Order agenda wouldn't be about control and tyranny, but about freedom, which they are systematically taking from us.

Yes, we want our utopia now, as Sinclair Lewis said, and we can have it, if we are brave enough to awaken, and be ready for it.

Utopia awaits us. Let us create our own blueprint for it, one that truly can achieve a better and more sustainable future for all, without being controlled. We can make what is imagined of a better world, very real, and it will be anything but unrealistic, which those who prefer a dystopian reality would like you to believe it is.

CHAPTER 31

Awaken To The Shadow

One does not become enlightened by imagining figures of light, but by making the darkness conscious.

- CARL JUNG

Every night, when I go to sleep, I die. Every morning, when I wake up, I am reborn.

- MAHATMA GANDHI

Let's imagine ourselves waking up in a much better world, having defeated the soulless agenda that was being forced upon us by tyrannical elites, and ask ourselves how are we reborn, as Gandhi said, and live differently than how we lived before?

The only way we can live differently is if we remember the errors of our past, because if we don't, as philosopher George Santayana said, "Those who cannot remember the past are condemned to repeat it." We can create our utopia if we truly want to, for, as we know, we are powerful beyond measure, and can create whatever we put our minds to. But, if we haven't learned from the mistakes of our past, we will, invariably, be condemned to repeat it, again and again, as history has shown us throughout time. So, how can we finally draw wisdom from our past to illuminate the present? We must, above anything else, be awake, conscious human beings, and aware of not just our foibles and weaknesses, but what Carl Jung called the "shadow". In order for us not to function from the negative or sinister aspects of our personality, and wreak havoc with the world and our humanity, we must know, as Jung said, that "everyone carries a shadow, and the less it is embodied in the individual's conscious life, the blacker and denser it is. At all counts, it forms an unconscious snag, thwarting our most well-meant intentions."

What that tells us is that no matter how "well-meant" our intentions are, even if they are for a utopian world, there is no doubt that until we make our shadow conscious, we will allow for darkness to find its way right back into whatever world we create, and the destruction will begin all over again. It is the shadow dominant people in power, from political leaders, health officials, the pharmaceutical industry, and people like Klaus Schwab and the global elites (who are aiming for global governance), that we must keep a very close watch on. If we don't identify the shadow lurking behind their (supposed), well-meant intentions for us, like the ones I've mentioned a few times, lest you forget, which includes owning nothing, having no privacy, and eating fake meat and crickets, we will once again, like other civilizations that fell before us, be steered towards the darker aspects of human nature, and see unethical behavior and corruption rise, which is already increasing exponentially. How blind are we not to think this could end in total destruction, and we will be one more civilization that collapsed from stupidity, ignorance, and complete unconsciousness. Unless people acknowledge their shadow, and integrate it properly, the "blacker and denser" it will become, as Jung said, and that's when you allow for those in power to act out your shadow for you, and become tyrannical, evil rulers. Just listen to those that are enforcing rules on us now, and ask yourself, are they trustworthy people, who show no signs of personality flaws, or mental disorders? For someone like Anthony Fauci to arrogantly laugh about what he calls the "Fauci effect" ("Anthony Fauci Describes the 'Fauci Effect,' Brags He 'Symbolize[s]' 'Truth' on Covid" 2022), tells you a lot about his inflated sense of importance, and a great need for admiration, which could be

considered the personality of a narcissist. In an article
in Psychology Today, "The Surprising Shadow Side of
a Narcissist", by Marilyn Wedge, Ph.D., it says, "Freud
thought that narcissism was not treatable by traditional
psychoanalysis. Later therapists found that the narcissist's
feelings of grandiosity and superiority are defenses that
protect a fragile and fragmented self. Underneath the defenses lies considerable pain, self-loathing, and fragmen-
tation of the self." If Fauci is a narcissist, which I think
many would say that he is, we should ask ourselves, "are
these the types of people who are in positions of authority
over us"? Perhaps a more important question would be,
"and we go along with what they tell us to do?!"

It's unbelievable how it takes an extreme abuse of
power for people to suddenly be horrified and shocked
by it and wonder how in the world it could have happened, but completely clueless as to how they were part of
creating the very monster that now controls them. If you
want to understand the manifestation of the shadow at its
most evil, think of Hitler. He was the personification of
the shadow at its darkest, and rose to power by millions of
people in Germany projecting their unembodied shadow
onto him. It was the mass psychosis of anti-Semitism that
became the perfect storm to derange the minds of not
only people in Germany, but millions all over the world
that were pro-Nazism, who not only accepted evil, but
even normalized it.

Hitler's disdain for the Jews, caused him to project his unconscious shadow onto them — the very darkness he was denying in himself. Here was a very mentally deranged, evil man, who looked anything but Aryan (blonde and blue eyed), and was obsessed with creating what he felt was a better world (his idea of utopia), dominated by racial, and physical perfection that he, himself, did not have. What he did have was a deep, hidden self-loathing (his shadow), and it is these types of fatal flaws that many people in positions of power can have, which fuels their insatiable hunger for more power. Although I am not a psychologist, and have not professionally analyzed people like Anthony Fauci, Klaus Schwab, Bill Gates, and Mark Zuckerberg, (they are the usual suspects, but I can assure you there are many more who are like them), I can see that they are deeply flawed men, psychologically, by how driven they are by their tremendous egos, and dystopian visions for our future world. And, from what I've studied and learned about the shadow over the years, I'm convinced it's the emotional blind spot of their shadow that is buried deep within, which causes them to behave as egomaniacal, narcissistic, and tyrannical as they do. They lack what Jung called, "the first test of courage on the inner way", which is to confront their own shadow, but they can't because they are, essentially, cowards who simply cannot face their soullessness. They seem to be hell-bent on using their power to project onto others all the insecurity, and pain they are denying within themselves, and by doing so, wish for a soulless world dominated by something like artificial intelligence that will take the place of human intelligence because, according to them, it is so limited. What fully integrated, non-fragmented person would wish for such a cold future like that? They may pretend they are creating a "better and more sustainable future for all", as they'd like us to believe, but, in fact, they are already hijacking our vision for a better future, one that genuinely aspires to be more utopian, and instead, very strategically laying the groundwork for a dystopian reality, they will control, every step of the way.

If we are to awaken, successfully, we must acknowledge the shadow, and how it will seep into our psyches no matter how many times we "die" or are "reborn", as Gandhi said in his quote, which I interpret as dying from what no longer serves us, and reborn into a new beginning of possibilities. We must be reborn differently than any other civilization before us that destroyed itself by succumbing to an overpowering shadow, and be fully aware of the destruction it can cause, which is the very evil we find ourselves in the grips of. We must consciously see it for what it truly is by mindfully practicing one of the most important of the Noble Truths of the Eightfold Path, "Right View", as I spoke about earlier, which is seeing the world and everything in it as it really is, not as we believe, or want it to be. And that means not, for a second, lack the courage to face the shadow that is trying to overpower us, and stop it before it destroys us, as it most certainly can, just like other civilizations were destroyed by dark forces they refused to see for what it really was. And, if the shadow remains unconscious, as Jung said, "until you make the unconscious conscious, it will direct your life and you will call it fate."

We cannot call this dystopian reality that these power mongers are deciding for us, fate, and accept that this was meant to be because they told us, or should I say, warned us that we will own nothing, have no privacy, and be happy, and once that happens, that will be our fate. No, it should never be, but it can. If we accept these psychotic lies, and normalize them, as evil was normalized during Nazi Germany (be aware of what we are now calling the "new normal"), we may very well find ourselves living out this miserable fate, but will be so entrenched in the mass formation psychosis that so many people seem to be suffering from, they won't even be able to admit it to themselves, and that's when real human emotions get replaced by a deadening of our soul, which seems to be exactly what the transhumanists want. You might feel, "who needs emotions anyway"? They're so messy, and get in the way of trying to deny what's really going on, so maybe we should just suck it up and start acting more like robots because, after all, we're heading towards becoming super-computers anyway!

We must awaken, dear reader, and continue to pull back the veils of illusion. There is no other way to overcome this darkness — this sinister, collective shadow that has taken hold of our world, and unless we want to accept it as our fate, we must resist it with all of our might, and light.

"As far as we can discern, the sole purpose of human existence is to kindle a light in the darkness of mere being."

— Carl Jung

CHAPTER 32

Resisting
The Singularity

Our sole responsibility is to produce something
smarter than we are; any problems beyond that are
not ours to solve...

- RAY KURZWEIL

The Singularity is Near: When Humans Transcend Biology

I set the date for the Singularity — representing a profound and disruptive transformation in human capability
— as 2045. The nonbiological intelligence created in
that year will be one billion times more powerful than all
human intelligence today.

- RAY KURZWEIL

The Singularity is Near: When Humans Transcend Biology

Fantastic Voyage: Live Long Enough
to Live Forever.

- RAY KURZWEIL

The Singularity is Near: When Humans Transcend Biology

Do you realize that if you fall into a black hole, you
will see the entire future of the Universe unfold in
front of you in a matter of moments and you will
emerge into another space-time created by the singularity of the black hole you just fell into?

- NEIL DEGRASSE TYSON

In futurist, Ray Kurzweil's book, *The Singularity Is Near:
When Humans Transcend Biology,* he writes that, "The
Singularity is a future period which the pace of technological
change will be so rapid, its impact so deep, that human life
will be irreversibly transformed. Although neither utopian
nor dystopian, this epoch will transform the concepts that
we rely on to give meaning to our lives, from our business

models to cycle of human life, including death itself. Understanding the Singularity will alter our perspective on the significance of our past and the ramifications of our future. To truly understand it inherently changes one's view of life in general and one's own particular life." Kurzweil goes on to say that he "regards someone who understands the Singularity and who has reflected on its implications for his or her own life as a singulatarian" (Kurzweil 2005).

I am not a "singulatarian", for the simple reason that I do not feel a need to "transcend the limitations of our biological bodies and brains", that Kurzweil says the Singularity will allow us to do, by "merging our biological thinking and existence with our technology, resulting in a world that is still human but that transcends our biological roots." So much of what Kurzweil lays out in *The Singularity is Near*, and his vision of what is "neither utopian nor dystopian" (then what is it?), boils down to, for me, that in order for us to be less limited, or should I say, more perfect, we must transfer our human intelligence onto artificial intelligence, because as Kurzweil says, "although impressive in many respects, the brain suffers from severe limitations." Ok, so we're limited. I get that. But, does that then mean if we don't prepare ourselves for the "accelerated pace of change" that Kurzweil warns us of in his book, "our human-created technology and its power is going to explode with unexpected fury, if one does not take care to follow its trajectory."

And how should we do that, Ray? If "our sole responsibility is to produce something smarter than we are, but "any problems beyond that are not ours to solve", as he says in his quote, then should we just assume and accept that our number one responsibility should be to produce something smarter than we are, but whatever happens after that is not a problem for us to deal with or solve? What if the "unexpected fury" of our "human created technology" is a type of explosion that is so catastrophic, artificial intelligence will cause human extinction, which apparently AI researchers have a concern about. In an article in Vox, "AI Disaster Won't Look Like The Terminator. It Will Be Creepier," a scientist lays out two possible scenarios, Dylan Mathews writes that Nate Soares, who runs the Machine Intelligence Research Institute, says, "The problem isn't that AI will suddenly decide we all need to die; the problem is that we might give it instructions that are vague or incomplete and that lead to the AI following our orders in ways we didn't intend" (Matthews 2019).

Here's the quote I shared earlier by Carl Jung, "Everyone carries a shadow, and the less it is embodied in the individual's conscious life, the blacker and denser it is. At all counts, it forms an unconscious snag, thwarting our most well-meant intentions." Do you know what my greatest concern is? It's not that our human created technology is going to explode with unexpected fury, it's that the people who are creating such powerful technology are not as awake and conscious as they should be to assume responsibility for the very things they're creating, like AI. How can you possibly say, as Kurzweil does, that any problems beyond producing something smarter than we are, are problems not for us to solve? How egregiously irresponsible is that!

He goes on to say in his book that, "although the Singularity has many faces, its most important implication is this: our technology will match and then vastly exceed the refinement and suppleness of what we regard as the best of human traits." Really? So, instead of us working on ourselves to be better human beings in our biological form, we want to create technology that has "the best of human traits" that transcends biological form? Why is it that these men, like Kurzweil, and Mark Zuckerberg, want to replace us and our universe with what they think is a better (more improved) version, but seem to show no regard for becoming better people (I guess Zuckerberg thinks he's a better person by suppressing free speech on Facebook and Instagram with censorship and cancel culture because he's superior to those with differing opinions than him, and calls what they say, "misinformation"). These futurists and their grandiose visions of what they think is human perfection has absolutely nothing to do with being an awake, conscious human being, and everything to do with being artificial or virtual. I guess the human form, and our universe is so repugnant to them, that is why they are trying to lead us towards an "AI disaster that won't look like the terminator. It will be creepier", as Dylan Matthews title says.

In the article, Matthews goes on to say that Nate Soares has argued a better analogy of what could go wrong with AI safety other than comparing it to the Terminator, by showing a scene from the animated movie, *Sorcerer's Apprentice*. It shows Mickey Mouse, who feels he needs help to fill a cauldron with water, take the sorcerer's cone shaped hat, and assume the power of the sorcerer. He enchants a broom (which represents AI) to help him fill the cauldron with buckets of water, but all hell breaks loose when the broom rebels and acquires a will of its own, overflowing the cauldron with water. And, when Mickey tries to destroy the AI broom by chopping it into pieces with an ax, it automatically rebuilds itself, creating hundreds of AI brooms that Mickey cannot control. It's interesting that Mickey Mouse represents everything that Disney wants to portray, like fun and happiness to "bring families together", as we've always thought of it to do. And here's sweet little Mickey, who seems perfectly well-intended to help fill the cauldron with water, but it's his ego that gets the best of him by believing he could be as mighty and powerful as the sorcerer, and by aiming his intention onto the (AI) broom to help assist him, that's when everything goes terribly wrong. There was nothing nefarious about Mickey's intentions, but, as we know, when the ego takes over, it can be very destructive, which is what happens when Mickey's ego becomes inflated, and he believes he could be as powerful as the sorcerer (this is the blind spot of the shadow). When the sorcerer appears and sees what Mickey has done, and that the cauldron has spilled over, creating what looks like a raging sea, it's the sorcerer who can split the water, like God commanded Moses to do so the Israelites could cross safely as they fled from the Egyptians. When Mickey looks up at the sorcerer with fear in his eyes, he hands him back his hat with a sheepish grin, like a child who has been caught doing something wrong. The sorcerer looks at him with silent scorn, and as Mickey walks away to go back to doing his job of filling the buckets of water himself, as he was supposed to do, the sorcerer hits him on his bottom with the broom, as if disciplining him like an adolescent.

I think it's a great metaphor to depict, not only what could go terribly wrong with AI, but how easily it can happen when man's ego gets in the way, fooling him to believe he's a mighty sorcerer, or can even play God. But, as the sorcerer shows Mickey, all too well, do not think you are more powerful than what is more powerful than you, even if you created it, because it can easily turn on you, and become catastrophic. *The Singularity Is Near,* lets us know that humans are playing God by creating artificial intelligence, not that Kurzweil says that those creating

AI suffer from a God complex. But, if you take the term, "God created man in his own image", (Genesis 1:27), I think we are at a very dangerous point with our (human created) technology, where man is, indeed, playing God, and creating machines to represent the new (improved) human, or should I say "transhuman". Perhaps these creators believe they are outdoing God (for those that even believe in a God because many futurists and transhumanists do not believe in God, and are atheists), and man will do a much better job at fixing the human limitations and imperfections that we have, and even transcend death by "transferring or resurrecting our minds onto supercomputers, allowing us to live forever", as Kurzweil believes we will do. This is how "our bodies will become incorruptible, immune to disease and decay." God never offered us that.

If you go by the term, "God created man in his own image", it is meant that humans are in the image of God in their moral, spiritual, and intellectual nature, so does that mean since we have failed so miserably in those areas, it's incumbent upon us to basically show God how imperfect he was in creating such imperfect humans, and prove that we can do a much better job at creating the perfect human, who will even be able to transcend its biology. See what a failure you are, God! You couldn't even do that, but we are now much more powerful than you ever were, or could be, and not only can we duplicate our intelligence onto machines, we never have to become ill or die, which you have caused us great suffering by creating us with such unthinkable imperfections. And, for anyone who still believes in this imperfect God as the all-powerful creator, you should know that the Singularity is near, and if you're not a singulatarian, you will continue to live as a pathetic, imperfect human, and how sad for you, especially if you go along with Klaus Schwab, and the global elites who want you to own nothing, have no privacy, and eat fake meat and crickets.

Dear (hopefully) awake reader, I seriously pray that you are aware of the Godless, and soulless future that awaits you if you do not ignite your very own biological power that you naturally have. If ever there was a time to prove how powerful you truly are, it is now. We have been brainwashed for the last two years that we are weak, and that our brilliantly designed bodies couldn't withstand a novel, man-made virus (yes, we also create things like bioweapons along with AI), and that our immune system is flawed because we are so imperfect, as God intended us to be, because remember, he, too, is imperfect, and we were made in his image. We were pressured, coerced, and terribly misled to believe we needed an experimental mRNA vaccine to make it all okay since our bodies are incapable of naturally producing an immune response, as our government, big pharma, and health officials want us to believe.

The Singularity may be near, but so is an awakened group of people, all over the world, who are undeniably powerful. They have had enough of thinking they are weak, and not the powerful humans that they truly are. They would never allow an artificial intelligence to take their place, not now, not ever. Kurzweil says that there are "Six Epochs of Evolution", and that the final epoch (6) is when "the universe wakes up", and that is when "patterns of matter and energy in the universe become saturated with intelligent processes and knowledge." According to Kurzweil, Epoch 5, which is before we get to when he thinks the universe will wake up, is when the "merger of technology and human intelligence takes place" and that means, "the methods of biology (including human intelligence) are integrated into the (exponentially expanding) human technology base." I can see why Kurzweil feels that being a singulatarian has been "an alienating and lonely experience for him because most people he encounters don't share his outlook." I wonder why!

I don't know you, Ray, and maybe one day we can meet and discuss your theories on the Singularity in person, but I don't believe the "universe will wake up" as you think that it will. No, I think the universe will wake up when human beings, with real, (not artificial) intelligence, wake up to realize they have much more to learn about themselves, and acknowledge that they have made some critical mistakes on this planet, which we still have time to repair. But can that partly be because we have been led to believe we are not as strong and powerful as we really are, and capable of so much more than we have realized about ourselves in human form? Kurzweil says in The Singularity that, "We have the means right now to live long enough to live forever." Yes, there will be "life-extending therapies from biotechnology and nanotechnology that will become available", as he mentions. But, he also says that, "most baby boomers won't make it because they are unaware of the accelerating aging process in their bodies and the opportunity to intervene" (Kurzweil 2005).

Is that what we should be most aware of? Aging and dying? It seems that is what we've become most afraid of. Perhaps we should live each day as though it were our last, and instead of seeking to remain immortal by becoming artificial, we should live by the words of Buddha who said, "Even death is not to be feared by one who has lived wisely." Living wisely is not giving our intelligence over to a machine, but empowering ourselves with a greater intelligence that will not allow us to destroy ourselves.

CHAPTER 33

The Omega Point

The future is more beautiful than all the pasts.

- PIERRE TEILHARD DE CHARDIN

We're a crowd, a swarm. We think in groups, travel in armies. Armies carry the gene for self-destruction. One bomb is never enough, the blur of technology. This is where the oracles plot their wars. Because now comes the introversion. Father Teilhard knew this, the omega point, a leap out of our biology. Ask yourself this question: Do we have to be humans forever?

- DON DELILLO, POINT OMEGA

The Omega Point is a term that was invented by the French Jesuit Catholic priest, and scientific mystic, Pierre Teilhard de Chardin, and means "a future time when everything in the universe will spiral towards a final point of divine unification" ("Omega Point" 2022). Although it is considered the final step before the Singularity takes place, which I spoke about in the previous chapter, I want to explore the Omega Point "as the place where both the physical and spiritual consciousness would unite. The place where the cosmos meets God", as Pierre Teilhard de Chardin described it.

I feel that so much of what the Singularity represents, seems devoid of God, or a Divine presence, and focuses primarily on man becoming a machine, even though Ray Kurzweil calls it a "spiritual machine", which I don't see what's spiritual about computers exceeding human intelligence. But, if we think of the universe spiraling towards a final point of unification, might it be a type of union where we merge with a supreme being, and become all that is, ever was, and will be. In the language of Scripture, it says that God is "drawing all things to Himself" (John 12:32), so that, in the end, "God will be all in all." However, for those that are not religious, or do not believe in a God, who, or what do they believe we will merge with at that final point of unification?

The Omega Point is both a spiritual belief, and a scientific speculation that everything in the universe is fated to spiral towards a final point of "divine" unification, so is this divine unification one with God, or "where the cosmos meets God", as Pierre Teilhard de Chardin believed it to be? If transhumanists, like Ray Kurzweil, believe that we will become "spiritual machines", then is that what will merge with God and the cosmos? It does seem challenging to remove God, or a Divine presence from this idea of reaching the Omega Point; when "the universe will spiral towards a final point of divine unification." Perhaps this is what man will grapple with as he decides what he feels we should become, or destined to be. Are we already divine beings, or are we destined to become "spiritual machines"? I guess time will tell, who, or what we will be, before we reach the Omega Point. Teilhard de Chardin viewed the universe as an evolutionary process which was constantly moving toward a greater complexity and higher levels of consciousness, so I'd like to think that as we move towards these higher levels of consciousness, we will continue to delve into areas that helps us understand how we can evolve as more conscious human beings before we reach that final point of unification. And, "even if we eventually cease to be humans in the near future, and computers will surpass our collective intellect, and our only way to maintain our place in the universe will be to merge with them" (Castillo 2011), we will have reached the highest level of consciousness before "the world ends with a whimper, not a bang", a line in T. S. Eliot's poem, The Hollow Men.

Eliot's poem, which "explores themes of religious confusion, despair, and the state of the world in disarray following the First World War" (Singh 2022) has much to analyze, and been interpreted over the years to mean everything from a civilization in decline, atrocities of war, a lack of faith in society, and spiritual emptiness. It is a timeless poem that will always speak to what troubles man's soul, and I think it is very befitting for the time we are in presently. There seems to be so much that is troubling man's soul right now, and could this be why there are those men, some of which I have mentioned in this book, who are not addressing what is stirring in their souls, but feel, instead, that it's best to overcome man's restless soul by annihilating it, and what better way to do that then to turn man into a machine. It is a cold proposition, at its core, but if we are constantly moving towards a greater complexity and higher levels of consciousness, as Pierre Teilhard de Chardin believed we are, we should consider the point of our evolution right now, which is already filled with tremendous complexity, requiring us to reach higher levels of consciousness to help us understand where we want our future evolution to go.

I would like to believe that before the world comes to an end, the universe will spiral towards a perfect, divine unification. But, before the Omega point happens, if it will, I feel we should take a deep, contemplative pause, and think about how we are preparing ourselves, consciously, to reach this divine unification in a way that will serve all of humanity. It doesn't seem as if futurists, like Kurzweil, or others who advocate transhumanism, feel that protecting the entire human race, is something to care about, because, as Kurzweil says, it is only those who cease "the opportunity to intervene the accelerating aging process in their bodies, and transcend human biology by becoming nonbiological intelligence, who will live long enough to live forever", and perhaps they will be the ones that will realize divine unification.

And, if you are not on board to begin this process of transcending human biology, and allow for something like getting microchipped, which will be the first step in becoming a supercomputer, good luck to you, not only reaching the Omega Point, but living beyond it, into infinity. It seems we are already being prepared to transcend our human biology, and when you hear that, in Sweden, thousands have already had microchips inserted into their hands (Savage 2019), what would make us think we aren't heading towards these points of transhuman evolution, like the Singularity, and right on schedule, as was planned. Even now, we are being told by the World Economic Forum founder, Klaus Schwab, who made it very clear what the future holds for us, when he explained the timetable for microchipping everyone by 2026, "At first we will implant them in our clothes…We will implant them in our brains or on our skin…In the end, maybe, there will be direct communication between our brain and the digital world" ("Klaus Schwab 2016 Implant Microchip, French with Engl. Translation" n.d.), and recently, Schwab and the global elites claim they want children microchipped too ("The World Economic Forum Wants Children Microchipped!" n.d.).

I know how horrifying this must sound, and I truly wish I could make it sound less horrific, but if you don't want the world to end with a "whimper", I encourage you to wake up, and do all that you can to "bang" on the doors of those who are ushering in this dystopian agenda, and let them know that you are resisting it with all of your human strength, which is mightier than you've ever imagined, or been told that it is. It's time, dear reader, to claim your sovereignty, and never again allow anyone, no matter their position of power, or authority, to tell you who you are, what you should or shouldn't do, what you should believe, what you should put inside your body, or to doubt, for one second, that you are not completely free, and fearless. If you want to be a human, or should I say, remain one, then fight for it, because this evil force that is upon us wants to suck your humanness right out of your miraculous body, and toss it aside for AI to take your place, which is extremely superior to you, or so these elites think, and want you to think.

These technocratic elites can't wait to replace you with artificial intelligence, and if you didn't already know, Flippy, the fast-food robot, just got hired in 100 restaurants to flip burgers better than you can (Ramirez 2022). Yes, "the future comes soon enough", as Einstein said, so wake up, and declare to this new future that you are ready for it, and get yourself even more ready to meet the challenges that will be thrown our way, because there will be many. We have much to do in the days ahead, and these changes, like wanting to usher in something like the Singularity, which again, is preparing us to transcend our human biology, will probably look very much like we've entered into a science-fiction reality beyond anything we've seen in a movie before.

John von Neuman, the "legendary" information theorist, says in his quote, "The ever-accelerating progress of technology and changes in the mode of human life give the appearance of approaching some essential singularity in the history of the race beyond which human affairs, as we know them, could not continue" ("One-a-Day Comments on AI Quotes in Forbes: Von Neumann" n.d.).

This proposes the question, "Does God intervene in human affairs", and if so, will God choose to allow our human affairs to continue? Whether there is a God, or not, perhaps there is a supreme intelligence that is more intelligent than we, or AI could ever be, and this supreme intelligence is orchestrating this evolutionary race towards the Omega Point of divine unification, to see what we will do next.

Carl Sagan said, "We are a way for the universe to know itself."

What will we do, moving forward, to help the universe know itself? Will we become the best of who we are in human form, or will we merge with computers who will surpass our collective intellect?

Stay awake to find out.

CHAPTER 34

EQ Consciousness

Where we have strong emotions,
we're liable to fool ourselves.

- CARL SAGAN

When we are awake, we are conscious, which means that we are aware. And, since there are different levels of awareness, that means there are different levels of consciousness. My awareness of something could be different than your awareness of it, which also means that either you, or I, could be completely unaware of something that the other is fully aware of, and it could be very important to know. If consciousness is awareness by the mind of itself, one's surroundings, and the world, it would seem that the more one is aware of oneself, surroundings, and the world, they are functioning from a greater degree of awareness, and that means they are more conscious.

Being a more conscious human being doesn't necessarily mean you are smarter, or more intelligent, it means that you have more self-awareness, and even though intelligent people may achieve higher results academically, not having self-awareness can interfere with their emotional intelligence (EQ), making them function from a lower EQ than someone who has a lower intelligence quotient (IQ). We live in a world that seems to place greater importance on IQ than EQ, and people who are well educated, and have degrees, are automatically assumed to be more intelligent than someone who is not. And, people who are well-educated, and have degrees, are usually the ones that go into professions that require those degrees, because, as we know, you cannot be a doctor, lawyer, investment banker, or a politician, unless you've had the required education to earn a place in the corporate, or political world. That means most professional positions of authority, or leadership, require a higher education, which indicates a higher level of intelligence, but nowhere in those highly-esteemed professions, does it require that you have emotional intelligence, and although there is an EQ test, The Global Emotional Intelligence Test, that uses 40 questions, they are "meant to be fun, and give you a guide to which EI areas you are doing well in and those which perhaps you need to focus on for development", according to The Global Emotional Intelligence Test website ("The EQ Test" n.d.).

Here are a few of the questions:

1. Trust by others
   is automatically given to me.
   is built through reliability and authenticity.

2. I always communicate in a way
   that everyone understands what I am saying.
   that seeks mutual understanding and full information sharing.

3. Others perspectives are always
   understood and sensitivity shown.
   clouding the issues and getting us off track.

4. When I see bias and intolerance I always
   challenge the initiating people.
   turn a blind eye and ignore it.

If I were to take just those four questions (out of 40), and answer them for Anthony Fauci, Bill Gates, Mark Zuckerberg, or Klaus Schwab, I would say that for the first question, trust seemed to just be "given to them", and was not "built through reliability and authenticity". Fauci never earned our trust, and not only lied to us about the safety of the Covid-19 vaccine, and it not preventing the virus or spreading it, as well as the masks not working, but he lied to Congress about Wuhan Lab Research (Browne 2021). There was absolutely zero building of trust with Fauci because there was never any true reliability and authenticity with him from the very beginning, and he really lost our trust when he debunked therapeutics, like Ivermectin and Hydroxychloroquine, that could have saved people's lives. For the second question, none of them communicates in a way that "seeks mutual understanding and full information sharing". Fauci, Gates, and Zuckerberg, don't need to seek our understanding of them, and have held information from the public that could be classified as criminal. For the third question about "others perspective" mattering to them, it doesn't seem that it does to any of these men, and they not only seem incapable of "showing sensitivity", but they are excellent at "clouding the issues and getting us off track." And for the fourth question, they are the ones that perpetuate "bias", and are completely "intolerant" of others with differing opinions, so therefore they "turn a blind eye and ignore" anyone who doesn't agree or go along with their narrative. As the king of censorship and cancel-culture, Mark Zuckerberg literally erases you off his social media platforms (Facebook & Instagram), if what you say goes against fact checker rules. I think he might have a sensitivity chip missing, which maybe his avatar on the Metaverse can make up for him.

I would say that they all fail miserably at Emotional

Intelligence, but because they are billionaires, extremely successful, and hold positions of authority, like Fauci, who was "the face of America's response to the Covid-19 pandemic" (Crane 2022), and the National Institute of Allergy and Infectious Diseases (NIAID), as well as the chief medical advisor to both President Trump, and Biden, until he stepped down, people seem to care less if a person in a position of power and authority, has emotional intelligence, if they even know what that is. Just because someone is well-educated, holds a position of authority, or has a list of credentials by their name, does not mean they should earn our trust automatically, especially if their self-awareness is grossly lacking. Do not confuse something like extreme confidence, as self-awareness, which can easily fool people to believe that someone who comes off self-assured is who you should put your complete trust in. We also know that someone who is charismatic, even if it's dark charisma, like Hitler was supposed to possess, which "generated a level of charismatic attraction that is almost without parallel" (Rees 2012), can win people over, blinding them to not only someone's emotional unintelligence, but also their shadow, which can intoxicate people to such a degree, they can succumb to something like "mass formation psychosis", which Dr. Robert Malone drew parallels of our time to the mentality developed among the German population in the 1920s and 1930s.

In the article, "His dark charisma", Laurence Rees

writes that "before WWI Hitler was a nobody, an oddball who could not form intimate relationships, was unable to debate intellectually and was filled with hatred and prejudice." I can't imagine how he could have possibly passed an emotional intelligence test, being that he was completely unable to perceive, use, understand, manage, and handle emotions, all of which makes for having emotional intelligence. If having EQ was actually a requirement to get into top schools, pursue higher education, become a professional in the field of law or medicine, as well as holding public office, I have no doubt there would be a staggering amount of people in professional positions of authority or leadership, who would never be where they are today. If only Hitler's complete lack of emotional intelligence was the very thing that exposed him for who he truly was, perhaps he never would have gotten as far as he did to be the evil monster he became. But the article does go on to say that "when Hitler spoke in the Munich bar halls in the aftermath of Germany's defeat in WWI, suddenly his weaknesses were perceived as strengths. His hatred chimed with the feelings of thousands of Germans who felt humiliated by the terms of the Versailles treaty and sought a scapegoat for the loss of the war. His inability to debate was taken as strength of character and his refusal to make small talk was considered the mark of a 'great man' who lived apart from the crowd" (Rees 2012). The scary thing about that is Hitler's lack of emotional intelligence worked in his favor because without self-awareness, or an ability to admit to his limitations, he relied on a type of fake confidence that fooled people into believing he was the "great man" they perceived him to be. And once he saw that he could win the crowds over, especially with his fiery charisma (when you see old newsreels of him, he always appears to be emotionally hot tempered, even full of rage, which is a clear sign that he was unable to manage his emotions), that was the perfect temperament in a leader that the people of Germany needed to ameliorate their humiliation of feeling defeated. And, with Hitler filled with so much hatred and prejudice already, he was the ideal person to find a scapegoat for the loss of the war, which he did with the Jews.

This does make me think that probably the only way for leaders to become tyrants, dictators, or any type of oppressor, they have to have a deep lacking of emotional intelligence, so much so, that their lack of not only self-awareness, but an empathic awareness of others, and the world, makes them unable to be a conscious, benevolent human being, which they cannot, or else they would never succeed in accomplishing what they are setting out to do, which is to control others to such a point, they can determine their fate for them. And that's exactly where we find ourselves today. The men that are controlling the world right now, like Bill Gates, Klaus Schwab, and all the global elites, are showing signs of a complete lack of emotional intelligence, and we are allowing for it, which is shocking. In as much as I can understand how someone with a personality defect, enlarged ego, or pronounced shadow, can be in a position of power or authority, I am still having an extremely hard time wrapping my head around how we could allow for this, and how so many people who you would think, they, themselves, have not only a high IQ, but also healthy EQ, are allowing for this to happen. It's as if they absolutely cannot accept that anyone who is in a legal position of authority (which can easily be corrupted), is capable of lying, and they have given over their trust to these untrustworthy people, like the people of Germany trusted a madman like Hitler to lead the way. It seems as if not only are we dealing with mass formation psychosis, but that the function of human consciousness has broken down and become so divided, it's making us function as if we have multiple personality disorders, which is why everything seems so crazy right now.

To think that it might get worse before it gets better, is a very hard pill to swallow, and I keep stressing how waking up is the only hope, I feel, that we have to get us through this extremely uncertain time, and connect us to a unity of consciousness that will bring us together in a way that we will be able to usher in, not a New World, ordered by elites who want to determine our fate for us, but Our New World, that has rid itself of those who want to control and govern us, and run our civilization into a precipitous decline. Let them go find another planet to inhabit (isn't that what you want, Elon Musk, with your SpaceX program getting us to the moon, and Mars?), and if they want it to be run by artificial intelligence, or "spiritual computers", they should. A world without (human) emotional intelligence, or consciousness, is a world that is empty and hollow, inhabited by hollow men, that T.S. Eliot writes about in his poem.

No, we will not let the world end with a whimper. We will let our voices be heard, loudly, until the whole world knows that we want our utopia now, and have the emotional intelligence needed for it.

CHAPTER 35

It Is Up To Us

You have no control over the hand that life deals you,
but how you play that hand is entirely up to you.

- VOLTAIRE

When we look back throughout history, we've seen periods where it seemed as if the world wasn't going to make it. According to a short film, "10 Times the Earth Was Almost Destroyed" n.d., "From crazy explosions to fast striking asteroids and even massive ice ages, planet Earth has had its life flash before its eyes a few times." There were some natural events that could have taken us down, but, if you go by the article, "15 Times The World Was Almost Completely Destroyed" (Opera News n.d.), many of them were man-made nightmares. There was the time in 1995 when the Cold War was over, and Russia's president, Boris Yeltsin, almost nuked America when he "opened a briefcase with the nuclear codes for the first time, and with ten minutes to figure out whether or not to nuke America, Yeltsin ultimately (and fortunately) got word that it was a science experiment he hadn't been warned about."

Then there was an incident in 1971, when "a teletype operator stuffed the wrong tape into an alert system machine", and instead of saying "this is only a test, it said that the president of the United States was about to broadcast an emergency alert 45 terrifying minutes later, NORAD", the North American Aerospace Defense Command, "realized their error" (Opera News n.d.).

And then, of course, there was one of the most remembered events in 1962, when the Cuban Missile Crisis almost caused a nuclear war. Regarded as "the closest we ever came to completely annihilating human existence, during a combination of missteps when an American air base guard activated the wrong alarm, which signaled WWIII from Wisconsin. The next day, America accidentally launched two missile tests in Russia because they had been scheduled before the crisis began." And, even now, Russian President Vladimir Putin has "raised the prospect of using nuclear weapons in the war he launched to destroy Ukraine" (Washington Post 2022).

If we were to think about how we would prefer a major catastrophe to happen, or even the world ending, (obviously, we don't want either to happen), but if we had to choose between a natural disaster, or a man-made one, which would we rather have? We know that mother earth, and the solar system, can behave in unpredictable ways that are out of our control, like in 1883 when hundreds of fragments from a comet (known as the Bonilla comet), narrowly missed Earth by 400 miles, and could have had an impact that would have been catastrophic. And in 1816, a volcano (Mount Tambora) in Indonesia, killed 71,000 people, livestock, and crops all around the world, causing a terrible famine (Opera News n.d.).

There have also been pandemics, like the Spanish Flu in 1918, which infected 500 million people, and killed 3.5% of the entire globe's population. But it's the man-made mistakes, I feel, that are harder to accept, especially if we know that someone has made a "combination of missteps", like the air base guard who activated the wrong alarm in the Cuban Missile Crisis that almost caused a nuclear war. We also need to consider the companies that are responsible for some of the biggest oil spills, like Union Oil Company, South Gulf Shipping Company, and Exxon, to name a few, as well as PG & E (Pacific Gas & Electric Company), which caused more than 1,500 California wildfires in the past six years, "California finds PG & E equipment responsible for massive Dixie Fire, burning nearly 1 million acres and destroying more than 1,300 homes" (Newburger 2022). We know, "To err is human", as poet Alexander Pope said. The remainder of that line is, "To forgive divine", but some might argue that forgiveness shouldn't be so easily given when human errors are too great, which brings to mind what

Ray Kurzweil said, "Our sole responsibility is to produce something smarter than we are; any problems beyond that are not ours to solve ..."

So, if something catastrophic were to happen, as I spoke about earlier, like the possibility of artificial intelligence causing human extinction, the real problem, according to Nate Soares, who runs the Machine Intelligence Research Institute, "isn't that AI will suddenly decide we all need to die; the problem is that we might give it instructions that are vague or incomplete and that lead to the AI following our orders in ways we didn't intend." Would we say to something as unimaginably horrific as that, "To err is human?" And, would we dare add to that, "To forgive divine?"

Have we reached a very dangerous point where we feel that we don't have to hold those accountable, who could, very possibly, be the reason why artificial intelligence could cause human extinction, and are we making light of what these people, like Kurzweil, Klaus Schwab, Bill Gates, and the rest of these transhumanists and global elites are telling us what they are planning to do, loud and clear? It's as if they're proudly warning us that human extinction is just around the corner, and we should get ready to lighten our load, by owning nothing.

These last, almost two and a half years, have really shown us that our humanity is hanging in a very delicate balance, and the reason for that seems to be man's inhumanity to man, if you add up everything that has transpired, including a pandemic that may very well have been caused by men, like Anthony Fauci, who was involved in "Gain-of-Function research", which supposedly was U.S. funded (Lerner et al. 2021), and "makes viruses more pathogenic or transmissible in order to study them, despite stipulations from U.S. funding agency that the money not be used for that purpose. Grant money for the controversial experiment came from the National Institutes of Health's National Institute of Allergy and Infectious Diseases, which is headed by Anthony Fauci." Were these just a "combination of missteps", which is how the Cuban Missile Crisis was described when an American air base guard activated the wrong alarm, which signaled WWIII from Wisconsin? And to add to that, Fauci withheld beneficial therapeutics from the public for Covid-19, like Ivermectin and Hydroxychloroquine, but instead, pushed the very dangerous drug, Remdesivir in its place. No misstep there, but a deliberate act of malintent, and possibly greed, if he got part of the action with Gilead Sciences, the giant manufacturer of antivirals, who struck a deal to supply the European Union with its drug, remdesivir, ("Remdesivir, given to Half of Hospitalized Covid Patients in U.S., Is Big Win for Gilead — Boosted by Taxpayers" 2021), which was developed with investment from the federal government, and is potentially worth more than $1 billion (Cohen and Kupferschmidt

2020). Remdesivir was given to half of hospitalized Covid patients in the U.S., even though one of its most known side-effects is acute kidney failure. According to an article in The Washington Free Beacon, Fauci's net worth doubled during Covid (Allen 2022).

It's so very troubling to think of how many men (including Bill Gates and Klaus Schwab), are behind what could be putting us, our country, and the world in extreme danger. I bring up emotional intelligence (EQ), because I feel it is what is deeply lacking in these men, and why they have such gross arrogance and greed, which puts all of us at risk because their visions are dystopian and anti-humanity (the blind spot of their shadow also contributes to it). I don't know of any woman behind these dystopian visions, but can't rule out the possibility there are any who are part of the World Economic Forum with Klaus Schwab, or that there are women who support the transhumanism movement. It's hard to imagine any woman would want to see her biological human form be replaced by artificial intelligence, which could never do one of the greatest human acts a woman can — give birth, and that would be participating in the end of procreation.

Planet Earth may have had its life flash before it's eyes a few times, but nothing compares to now when our advanced technology, coupled with people who are very powerful, and extremely wealthy, are in cahoots with one another to usher in something very ominous like a New

World Order, and transhumanism. So, I ask you, dear reader, what are we going to do about that? To awaken, is to emerge from a kind of slumber that has allowed us to tolerate, even accept heinous things to occur in the past, like Nazi Germany, and the Holocaust, and yet, even if we temporarily wake up from the horror of it all, and rub sleep from our eyes, or say "never again", here we are facing the danger of unconsciousness all over again. And that is when evil rears its ugly head because it knows exactly when we are asleep, and those that embody evil are the very ones that know, precisely, how to prey on our weaknesses, by wearing us down, and fooling us to do exactly as they say.

We must stop doing what they say, now! Do not comply, or go along with one more thing they say, or mandate, or else our life on planet earth will be flashing right before our eyes, only this time, it could be for real.

CHAPTER 36

Our New World

I shall create a new world for myself.

- FREDERIC CHOPIN

A hundred struggle and drown in the breakers.
One discovers the new world. But rather, ten times
rather, die in the surf, heralding the way to that new
world, than stand idly on the shore.

- FLORENCE NIGHTINGALE

Orwell's '1984' convinced me, rightly or wrongly,
that Marxism was only a quantum leap away from
tyranny. By contrast, Huxley's 'Brave New World'
suggested that the totalitarian systems of the future
might be subservient and ingratiating.

- J. G. BALLARD

What about the New World Order, sounds appealing to you? Even if we didn't know about the sinister intentions of those who want to bring in the New World Order, having the word "order", as part of the phrase, which means, "a statement made by a person with authority that tells someone to do something : an instruction or direction that must be obeyed" ("Order Definition & Meaning | Britannica Dictionary" n.d.), should not only make you nervous, but immediately cause you to ask, "what the hell is that?"

For any of us with a sound, "Right View" mind, we know that when we hear someone in a position of authority say, the "New World Order", we need to pay close attention. This was said by an Australian health official, Dr. Kerry Chant, when she answered a journalist's question about whether "contact-tracing" would be used once the country reopened. Although millions of people heard her say it, it's become predictable, lately, for the government and health officials to downplay, or minimize what they've said, if it's questioned (remember what it's called when you question authority), and they instantly relegate it to one more conspiracy theory, which, at this point, makes what is being questioned that much more valid to be questioned. "Dr. Kerry Chant caused a stir amongst conspiracy theorists when she referred to ongoing Covid restrictions as a 'new world order' necessity" (Hancock 2021). And, even when she answered the journalist's question about whether contact-tracing would be used once the country reopened, she answered, "We will be looking at what contact-tracing looks like in the new world order." For Dr. Chant to say, not only, "New World Order", but also "contact-tracing", which is used in China, a communist country that seems to have its own vision for a New World Order, even though "the Chinese leadership has not offered an explicit description of the world order it would like to see emerge" (Rolland 2020) again, we should pay very close attention. Contact-tracing means cell phones are used to collect information on all of the people you have come into contact with while testing positive for Covid, as well as, all of the places you have been, but according to an article in The Conversation, "Corona Virus Contact Tracing Poses Serious Threats To Our Privacy", which "is laborious and error-prone because it is dependent on memory, interviews and detective work." Prime Minster, Justin Trudeau, has considered using it in Canada, but the article goes on to say, "before the Canadian government makes decisions that infringe on civil liberties through widespread digital surveillance, we need to think about the concessions we make during a time of crisis. Crises have long been used as an opportunity by governments and corporations to infringe on civil liberties in the name of public safety" (Mauro 2020).

That means if we are going to be in a constant state of a health emergency, every time a new virus makes a debut, and the FDA decides to use EUA (Emergency

Use Authorization), something like contact-tracing could very well become one more mandate we will be forced to accept in the "new normal" that is being thrust upon us. When people questioned what Dr. Chant meant by using the term, "New World Order", the quickest way to make light of it was to say, "While some acknowledge that Dr. Chant's 'innocent turn of phrase' signified nothing more than a clumsy choice of words, dozens of conspiracy theorists took to social media to make unfounded claims about what the incident 'clearly means' in terms of the NOW debate" (Hancock 2021). Is there a "debate" about the New World Order because I haven't heard a word about it. Maybe it's being debated amongst the global elites, which means we have nothing to say in the matter, so whatever "claims" we might make about what they think the incident "clearly means", they will be viewed, automatically as "unfounded", therefore, conspiracy theories. Can you see how the game is played?

How much more gas-lighting do we need to hear, to get how the global elites are planting the seeds of their New World Order takeover, but when it's questioned, they quickly pretend that it's not, at all, what we think (and know) it is, and will say, every single time you question anything that someone in a position of authority says, boom, you are a conspiracy theorist! Does it not offend or insult you that these elites truly think you are stupid, and so beneath them, they can lie straight to your face that what they are saying, is not what they said, but it's you that heard it incorrectly, which not only makes you a conspiracy theorist, but even an extremist, or worse, a domestic terrorist. As I have said, these are very dangerous times, and in as much as I'd like to say, as Charles Dickens said in *A Tale of Two Cities*, "It was the best of times, it was the worst of times", if we don't wake up fast, it will only be the worst of times.

The New World Order is not Our New World, and we must claim our world as we wish it to be. Any time something of extreme importance is not realized, there is an exact reason for it, and I believe, it is the people that did not rise up to "contend with an unconscious force which can block, betray, or countermand almost any conscious intention of the collectivity", as science fiction author Frank Herbert said. We are not resisting this force, this evil, that wants to block, betray, and countermand our conscious intention to create Our New World, and we must for our civilization to survive.

We are in the midst of a war of the worlds, and I don't mean the movie of that title, *The War of the Worlds*, which is a science fiction novel by H. G. Wells. But, it does have a strong message that could be applied to what I believe is a spiritual war we are battling, over which new world, ours, or the ones who want us to obey their order that they will rule our universe. Wells' book explores the extremes of what is possible under evolution and natural selection, and its message, resonant to our existential plight, which is, "compared to humans, the Martians are highly advanced in their technology, suggesting that their evolutionary history is also longer than that of humans" (Wells 1986). Although our war is not with Martians (even though the global elites act alien, as if from another planet, terrorizing ours), we are fighting those that want to use advanced technology against us, and we must resist them so they don't take us over, and usher in their New World Order, obliterating the vision for Our New World that will not be ruled by advanced technology that can destroy our civilization, but by a higher consciousness realized by human intelligence, to advance our evolution towards greater possibilities. Our New World will not use force, coercion, gas-lighting, or any type of manipulation or control that threatens man's freedom, in any way. In Wyoming Law Journal, Frank. E. Holman writes, "American Freedom faces many perils and many threats. It is no mere matter of emotion of rhetoric to say that our individual freedoms and our form of government are challenged as never before. Some would doubtless say that Communism is the greatest threat to American freedom. Certainly, we have tolerated the high priests of this subversive and atheistic ideology in many places, in our schools, and in our colleges, in the professions and in business, and in the policy echelons of the Federal Government and in the United Nations." Holman, who was

known for his effort to amend the United States Constitution to limit the power of treaties and executive agree-
ments, wrote this in 1953, which explains why he believed
so strongly in American freedom. He continues in his
article to say, "Our American Freedom is supposed to be
safeguarded by our Constitution and Bill of Rights, but
during the last twenty years many Americans have given
no service at all or only lip service to the preservation of
our basic freedoms. Instead of devoting ourselves to the
security of our form of government and our fundamental freedoms thereunder — we have devoted ourselves
to various forms of social and economic security." What
Holman said in 1953, could easily be about the threats of
our freedom today, and when he uses this quote by Som-
erset Maugham, it really hits home to what we are facing
right now:

"If a nation values anything more than freedom,

it will lose its freedom.

And if it is money and comfort that it values more

it will lose those too."

Yes, the world was almost completely destroyed many times, and the possibility of communism being the greatest threat to American freedom, is something we could be facing more than ever before. But there does come a point when all of the things that have been threatening us for as long as they have, one day, those threats turn into reality, and that reality could be ours, if we don't fight for the kind of new world that is free of any threat to our freedom, and human evolution. We may not have reached our annihilation point, but when you hear about how the transhumanism movement is "no longer about abstract theoretical musings, but are being embedded into emerging technologies at organizations like Google, Apple, Tesla and SpaceX", which I discussed in an earlier chapter, and the phrase, New World Order, is being said across the globe by health officials, and heads of state, as though it is, in fact, our new reality, then it does make you wonder if we have reached that very crucial time in our existence where we could become extinct, sooner than we know.

So, dear reader, what are we to do? Are we going to remain asleep, or are we going to wake up with a vengeance, and fight for what rightfully belongs to us – Our New World. But we must create it, quickly, and not the way robots and artificial intelligence are created. That is man creating machines that can not only misinterpret him, but outsmart him. We are not humans fighting Martians with advanced technology, as was the story in

The War of the Worlds. We are a civilization at war with itself, divided amongst those who want to mastermind our destruction with advanced technology, and those that will lead us towards a Divine Unification, as Pierre Teilhard de Chardin believed, and we will get there with the greatest power we have, our human consciousness.

Never underestimate the power of the minds that are most conscious, for the power of the conscious mind is beyond our imagination.

CHAPTER 37

We Are Awake, Now What?

We have never arrived.
We are in a constant state of becoming.

- BOB DYLAN

To arrive was to die a little.

- ANTHONY POWELL

Was I sleeping, while the others suffered? Am I sleeping now? Tomorrow, when I wake, or think I do, what shall I say of today?

- SAMUEL BECKETT

My dear reader, thank you for being on this journey of awakening. I know it's been a hellish one, and I commend you for having the strength and stamina to withstand the extreme difficulties you have endured. You are remarkable, and I feel blessed that we travelled this arduous path together, for we could not have done it alone. When I was weak, you were strong, and when you weakened, I showed you the strength you showed me. And, even with those we never met, we felt deeply connected when we saw each other cry out on social media, before the controllers found us, and censored what we had to say. While we could, we held onto each other's words, as if they were exactly what we needed to hear; to get through one more day of the madness. We united, even while they tried to tear us apart. We found truth, even when they told us lies. And we never once caved, even when it got to be too much, and we were convinced that the Apocalypse was upon us.

We chose to be awake because it was always a choice. How easy would it have been for us to join those that pretended life was still the same, but we knew damn well, it wasn't. They turned the other way because they were afraid to face the unbearable truth that life, as we knew it to be, will never be the same again. No, they just could not accept it, so they did everything they were told to do, and believed if they did, the world would return to what it once was, but it could not. Sadly, many of them are not here anymore, and many more of them will become ill, or die, because they put poison in their bodies, until it could no longer withstand the bioweapon they chose to be injected with. How tragic that they did not trust their miraculous immune system to fight off a virus that was man made. We tried to warn them, but they refused to listen, or accept what we were saying. Many of them vilified us, called us names, kept us from loved ones, and even tried to cancel our very existence. But they could not.

So, here we are, dear reader, alive and awake, in Our New World that we believed was possible all along. Nobody "ordered" it. We created it, together. All of us that had the courage to awaken. It is not an artificial world, nor is it virtual. It is very, very real. And, in this new world of ours, we are free, and we own what is rightfully ours, and we eat what we want, and no, we do not eat bugs. Yes, we are free because sovereignty is our birthright. Nobody gave it to us, and nobody can take it away. We have always known that nobody owns us. Nobody controls us. Nobody tells us what to think. Nobody tells us what we can and cannot say. Nobody tells us what to do with our bodies. Nobody intimidates us with fear. Because we are the free ones. We have been free this whole time, even though they watched and tracked us with their surveillance, and knew what we were doing, and where we were going, and what we were posting, and buying, and saying. And yet, we remained free, because freedom is a state of mind, and no one can crawl inside our heads, and steal it from us. They still want our freedom, desperately, but we always knew that even if we were trapped inside a jail cell, alone, they still could not take our freedom from us because freedom cannot be owned by anyone other than the one who holds it deep inside their soul, and that is where they cannot go, inside the soul, which is where they are most afraid to be. They are afraid to venture into the depths of their being. They are afraid to feel emotions that make them feel vulnerable, or out of control.

That is why they love machines because they cannot feel. And yet, they want to program them to simulate human emotions, even pain. But, do they not know that is how they can be tricked? The machines they are creating can turn on them, and own them, and tell them what to do, and what to think, and where to go, or worse, prevent them from going where they wish to go because they will be imprisoned by the machines they have created. Their machines will not be benevolent, a quality that those who want to destroy us, don't value. They don't value human qualities like benevolence, and compassion. They are too busy focusing on how imperfect humans are, and while we live in Our New World, they are busy creating their technology to match what they think is "the best of human traits", and vastly exceed them, but they are very wrong about what they think the best of our human traits are. Some of our best human traits are honesty, integrity, courage, self-awareness, wholeheartedness, and empathy. They are qualities that define who we are as human beings, and Aristotle was right when he said, "Men acquire a particular quality by constantly acting in a particular way." We "acquired" those qualities by how we acted, and we continued to act with those qualities when we were being coerced, manipulated, and threatened. Never did we stop being self-aware, honest, courageous, wholehearted, and empathic, even when they tried to wear us down, over and over again. And what qualities did those who had authority over us, and tried to control us, possess? Did they have any of those best qualities? No. They possessed the very opposite of man's best traits, and instead they acted with the worst of our human qualities, which are: controlling, judgmental, dishonest, aggressive, predatory, narcissistic, vindictive, greedy, egocentric, unforgiving, and always needing to be right.

Our New World is where we exist with the very best of our human traits. We have no need for a machine, or artificial intelligence, to possess the qualities that only we can possess, for there will never be a machine that can replace us, unless we allow for it, and we are far too intelligent for that to happen. Through tremendous hard work, we have arrived in Our New World, but make no mistake about it, the elites will still try to "order" their new world, and force it upon us. They will not rest until we are replaced by supercomputers and robots, which the transhumanists will continue to aim for, until that day comes. Don't they realize that if they did manifest their dystopian world, Siri, or Mark Zuckerberg's new robot, Jarvis, might decide they are smarter without them, and they could cease to exist.

We, dear awakened ones, never existed just to exist. We exist to awaken to a higher state of consciousness, but still have a long way to go on our journey of spiritual evolution. Let us not stop here, for there are even higher states of consciousness for us to realize, which no machine will ever be able to.

Are you ready to awaken more?

"Love is the most universal, the most tremendous and the most mystical of cosmic forces. Love is the primal and universal psychic energy. Love is a sacred reserve of energy; it is like the blood of spiritual evolution."

- PIERRE TEILHARD DE CHARDIN

The Spirit of the Earth

References

Chapter 1 - Welcome To Awaken

Butter, Michael. 2020. "There's a Conspiracy Theory That the CIA Invented the Term 'Conspiracy Theory' – Here's Why." The Conversation. March 16, 2020. https://theconversation.com/theres-a-conspiracy-theory-that-the-cia-invented-the-term-conspiracy-theory-heres-why-132117.

Ryan, Benjamain and Matt Lavietes. 2022. "Monkeypox Is Being Driven Overwhelmingly by Sex between Men, Major Study Finds." NBC News. https://www.nbcnews.com/nbc-out/out-health-and-wellness/monkeypox-driven-overwhelmingly-sex-men-major-study-finds-rcna39564.

"Vaccines ProCon.org." 2019. Procon.org. 2019. https://vaccines.procon.org.

Chapter 2 - Are You Ready To Awaken?

Plandemic. 2021. www.simonandschuster.com. https://www.simonandschuster.com/books/Plandemic/Mikki-Willis/9781510765542.

"Glutathione: The Most Powerful and Potent Antioxidant That Detox ifies the Entire Body." n.d. www.doctorsformulas.com. https://www.doctorsformulas.com/en/category/glutathione-the-most-powerful-and-potent-antioxidant-that-detoxifies-the-entire-body.htm.

Crump, Andy, and Satoshi Ōmura. 2011. "Ivermectin, 'Wonder Drug' from Japan: The Human Use Perspective." Proceedings of the Japan Academy. Series B, Physical and Biological Sciences 87

(2): 13–28. https://doi.org/10.2183/pjab.87.13.

Baragona, Justin. 2021. "Fauci Implores People to Stop Taking Horse Drug to Prevent COVID: 'Don't Do It!'" The Daily Beast, August 29, 2021, sec. media.
https://www.thedailybeast.com/dr-fauci-implores-people-to-stop-taking-horse-drug-to-prevent-covid-says-dont-do-it.

"Rand Paul Confronts Fauci with Video of His Own Past Statements on Natural Immunity." n.d.
www.youtube.com. Accessed September 21, 2022.
https://www.youtube.com/watch?v=JAXKQmVrf0k.

Browne, Ed. 2021. "Fauci Was 'Untruthful' to Congress About Wuhan Lab Research, New Documents Appear To Show."
https://www.congress.gov/117/meeting/house/114270/docu ments/HHRG-117-GO24-20211201-SD004.pdf.

Chapter 3 - What You Need To Know About Awakening

"Joe Biden Gets COVID - 'You're Not Going to Get COVID If You Have These Vaccinations...'" n.d.
www.youtube.com. Accessed September 22, 2022.
https://www.youtube.com/watch?v=rNyZm6A0OfQ.

American Medical Association. 2016. "Informed Consent."
https://www.ama-assn.org/delivering-care/ethics/informed-consent.

Chapter 4 - Waking Up To A Virtual Reality And Transhumanism

Gleiser, Marcelo. 2014. "The Transhuman Future: Be More than You Can Be." NPR, June 11, 2014, sec. Culture.
https://www.npr.org/sections/13.7/2014/06/11/320961912/ the-transhuman-future-be-more-than-you-can-be#:~:text=Trans humanism%2C%20according%20to%20the%20dictionary.

Wikipedia Contributors. 2019. "Transhumanism." Wikipedia. Wikimedia Foundation. November 18, 2019.
https://en.wikipedia.org/wiki/Transhumanism.

Caldera, Camille. 2020. "Fact Check: Americans Won't Have Micro-

chips Implanted by End of 2020." USA TODAY. August 1, 2020.
https://www.usatoday.com/story/news/factcheck/2020/08/01/fact-
check-americans-will-not-receive-microchips-end-2020/5413714002/.

"Biden Signs CHIPS Act, Sending $53 Billion to US Chipmakers."
2022. Newsnetdaily.com. August 9, 2022.
https://newsnetdaily.com/biden-signs-chips-act-sending-53-bil
lion-to-us-chipmakers/.

Breuninger, Kevin. 2022. "Biden Signs China Competition Bill to
Boost U.S. Chipmakers." CNBC.
https://www.cnbc.com/2022/08/09/biden-to-sign-chips-act-china-
competition-bill.html.

DeMattia, Nico. 2022. "Biden Signs CHIPS Bill to Boost US Microchip
Makers, Jumpstart Car Production." The Drive. August 9, 2022.
https://www.thedrive.com/news/biden-signs-chips-bill-to-boost-
us-microchip-makers-jumpstart-car-production.

Dorisca, Samantha. 2022. "Elon Musk Will Reportedly Be Implanting
Microchips into Humans as Early as This Year." AfroTech. January
6, 2022.
https://afrotech.com/elon-musk-micro-chips-humans-neuralink.

Adl-Tabatabai, Sean. 2022. "Klaus Schwab's Nazi Roots Explain the
'Great Reset' Agenda." News Punch. March 30, 2022.
https://newspunch.com/klaus-schwabs-nazi-roots-explain-the-
great-reset-agenda/.

Chapter 5 - Why Awakening Is So Important Right Now

Greene, Jenna 2021. "Wait What? FDA Wants 55 Years to Process
FOIA Request over Vaccine Data."

Reuters, November 18, 2021, sec. Government.
https://www.reuters.com/legal/government/wait-what-fda-wants-
55-years-process-foia-request-over-vaccine-data-2021-11-18/.

Chapter 6 – Why Ignorance Is Not Bliss

Goel, Avijit 2020. "Dr Cover-Up: Tedros Adhanom's Controversial
Journey to the WHO." ORF. Accessed September 26, 2022.
https://www.orfonline.org/expert-speak/dr-cover-up-tedros-adha

noms-controversial-journey-to-the-who-65493/.

Sinsabaugh, Annie and Meghna Chakrabarti. 2021. "How the 'Disin formation Dozen' Spreads Vaccine Misinformation Online." www.wbur.org. https://www.wbur.org/onpoint/2021/08/06/vac cine-misinformation-and-a-look-inside-the-disinformation-dozen.

"ACTIVIST VERA SHARAV'S THOUGHT 'the WAR against HUMANI TY' TOLD by a HOLOCAUST SURVIVOR [ENG]." n.d. www.youtube.com. Accessed September 26, 2022. https://www. youtube.com/watch?v=ad10Y8sKgWM.

Chapter 7 – Understanding Our Fears

Chiu, David. 2020. "Jonestown: 13 Things You Should Know about Cult Massacre." Rolling Stone. May 30, 2020. https://www.rolling stone.com/feature/jonestown-13-things-you-should-know-about-cult-massacre-121974/.

"No Lockdowns, No Mask Mandate: Sweden as a Case Study in What to Do (and Not Do) during a Pandemic." n.d. KCRW. https://www.kcrw.com/news/shows/press-play-with-madeleine-brand/edu-coronavirus-crime-food/sweden-covid.

Skopec, Robert. 2020. "Coronavirus Is a Biological Warfare Weaon." www.heraldopenaccess.us. December 31, 2020. https://www.heraldopenaccess.us/openaccess/coronavirus-is-a-biological-warfare-weapon

"Big Brother and Other Terms from '1984.'" 2019. Center for the Arts. October 31, 2019. https://cfa.gmu.edu/news/2019-10/big-brother-and-other-terms-1984.

Shriver, Lionel. 2021. "Breastfeeding Is Now Chestfeeding: Why Are the Language Police Trying to Wipe out Women?" www.thetimes.co.uk, sec. news review. https://www.thetimes.co.uk/article/breastfeeding-is-now-chestfeeding-why-are-the-lan guage-police-trying-to-wipe-out-women-wfqmws0j0.

Chapter 8 – Mindfulness And Awakening

Wehrwein, Peter. 2011. "Astounding Increase in Antidepressant Use

by Americans." Harvard Health Blog. October 20, 2011.
https://www.health.harvard.edu/blog/astounding-increase-in-antidepressant-use-by-americans-201110203624.

Chapter 9 – The Power Of Metacognition

Adair, Cam. 2021. "The Negative Effects of Video Games - 12 Symptoms." Game Quitters. July 6, 2021.
https://gamequitters.com/negative-effects-of-video-games/.

Joshi, Shamani. 2022. "The Metaverse, Explained for People Who Still Don't Get It."www.vice.com.March 15, 2022.
https://www.vice.com/en/article/93bmyv/what-is-the-metaverse-internet-technology-vr.

Atchison, Amy, and Shauna Shames. 2020. "Are We Living in a Dystopia?" The Conversation. April 29, 2020.
https://theconversation.com/are-we-living-in-a-dystopia-136908.

Chapter 10 – The Signs Of Awakening

Auken, Ida. 2016. "Welcome to 2030: I Own Nothing, Have No Privacy and Life Has Never Been Better." Forbes. Accessed September 30, 2022.
https://www.forbes.com/sites/worldeconomicforum/2016/11/10/shopping-i-cant-really-remember-what-that-is-or-how-differently-well-live-in-2030/?sh=2a5dc66c1735.

Chapter 11 – What To Be Aware Of In Your Awakening

"Red Pill and Blue Pill." 2020. Wikipedia. June 9, 2020.
https://en.wikipedia.org/wiki/Red_pill_and_blue_pill.

LaFraniere, Sharon. 2022. "Walensky, Citing Botched Pandemic Response, Calls for C.D.C. Reorganization." The New York Times, August 17, 2022, sec. U.S.
https://www.nytimes.com/2022/08/17/us/politics/cdc-rochelle-walensky-covid.html.

"Dr. Vladimir Zev Zelenko 05/23/22." 2022.
www.youtube.com. Accessed September 26, 2022.
https://www.youtube.com/watch?v=cwXV_rdxx9k.

Chapter 13 – The Great Awakening Initiation

"The First Great Awakening: Religious Revival and American Independence - Video & Lesson Transcript." n.d. **Study.com**. https://study.com/academy/lesson/the-first-great-awakening-religious-revival-and-american-independence.html.

O'Gieblyn, Meghan. 2017. "God in the Machine: My Strange Journey into Transhumanism." **The Guardian**, April 18, 2017, sec. Technology. https://www.theguardian.com/technology/2017/apr/18/god-in-the-machine-my-strange-journey-into-transhumanism.

Zola, Andrew. 2021. "What Is the Singularity?" **SearchEnterpriseAI**. https://www.techtarget.com/searchenterpriseai/definition/Singularity-the.

Auken, Ida. 2016. "Welcome to 2030: I Own Nothing, Have No Privacy and Life Has Never Been Better." **Forbes**. Accessed September 30, 2022. https://www.forbes.com/sites/worldeconomicforum/2016/11/10/shopping-i-cant-really-remember-what-that-is-or-how-differently-well-live-in-2030/?sh=2a5dc66c1735.

Chapter 14 - Staying On The Path Of Awakening

"**The Corona Scandal** - Reiner Fuellmich Is Suing the Promoters of the 'Corona Panic' (the Leader of WHO Adhanom, Drosten, & Wieler) for 'Crimes against Humanity.'" Accessed September 26, 2022. https://usercontent.one/wp/www.ooc.one/wp-content/uploads/2020/10/The-Corona-Scandal-Crimes-Against-Humanity-v3.pdf.

Reuters. 2021. "Jennifer Aniston Defends Cutting Ties with Unvaccinated Friends." Reuters, August 6, 2021, sec. Lifestyle. https://www.reuters.com/lifestyle/jennifer-aniston-defends-cutting-ties-with-unvaccinated-friends-2021-08-06/.

National-Times-Australia. 2021. "Pfizer Confirms COVID-Vaccinated People Can 'Shed' Spike Proteins and Harm the Unvaccinated." National Times Australia. June 26, 2021. https://www.nationaltimesaustralia.com/health/pfizer-confirms-covid-vaccinated-people-can-shed-spike-proteins-and-harm-the-unvaccinated/.

Philadelphia, The Children's Hospital of. 2021. "Feature Article: Viral Shedding and COVID-19 — What Can and Can't Happen." www.chop.edu. June 1, 2021. https://www.chop.edu/news/feature-article-viral-shedding-and-covid-19-what-can-and-can-t-happen.

"COVID-19 Vaccines, Irregular Periods and Spike Protein Shedding." n.d. www.nebraskamed.com. Accessed September 26, 2022. https://www.nebraskamed.com/COVID/the-covid-19-vaccines-irregular-periods-and-spike-protein-shedding.

Mandavilli, Apoorva, and Roni Caryn Rabin. 2021. "Pregnant Women Get Conflicting Advice on Covid-19 Vaccines." The New York Times, January 28, 2021, sec. Health. https://www.nytimes.com/2021/01/28/health/pregnant-women-covid-vaccines.html.

Chapter 17 - Defining Your Purpose As You Awaken

Bauer, Rebecca. 2021. "If Not for Climate, Then Why Is Bill Gates Buying so Much Farmland?" 2021. AFN. August 27, 2021. https://agfundernews.com/gates-if-not-for-climate-then-why-is-bill-buying-up-so-much-farmland.

"Bill Gates: Let Them Eat Fake Meat!" n.d. Children's Health Defense. https://childrenshealthdefense.org/defender/bill-gates-fake-meat/.

Chapter 19 – What Being Awake Does For Humanity

Kurzweil, Ray. 2001. The Age of Spiritual Machines : How We Will Live, Work and Think in the New Age of Intelligent Machines. New York ; London: Texere.

Chapter 20 – Living In A Parallel Universe

Wikipedia Contributors. 2019. "Parallel Universes in Fiction." Wikipedia. Wikimedia Foundation. September 8, 2019. https://en.wikipedia.org/wiki/Parallel_universes_in_fiction.

Galimova, Rezida Maratovna, Igor Vyacheslavovich Buzaev, Kireev Ayvar Ramilevich, Lev Khadyevich Yuldybaev, and Aigul Fazirovna Shaykhulova. 2019. "Artificial Intelligence—Developments in Medicine in the Last Two Years." Chronic Diseases and Translational Medicine 5 (1): 64–68. https://doi.org/10.1016/j.cdtm.2018.11.004.

"Event 201, a Pandemic Exercise to Illustrate Preparedness Efforts." 2019. Event 201.
https://www.centerforhealthsecurity.org/our-work/exercises/event201/.

Chapter 21 – A Conscious Civilization

Nickelsburg, Monica. 2017. "Bill Gates Invests in Veggie Burger That 'Bleeds' like Beef to Feed the Masses and Save the Planet." GeekWire. August 1, 2017.
https://www.geekwire.com/2017/bill-gates-invests-veggie-burger-bleeds-like-beef-feed-masses-save-planet/.

Clark, Mitchell. 2022. "Satellite-To-Phone Companies Are Thrilled about SpaceX and T-Mobile, Actually."
The Verge. Accessed September 27, 2022.
https://www.theverge.com/2022/8/27/23324128/t-mobile-spacex-satellite-to-phone-technology-ast-lynk-industry-reactions-apple.

Wagner, Paul. 2019. "Scientists Keep Warning about the Dangers of 5G; Will We Listen?" Gaia. Accessed September 27, 2022.
https://www.gaia.com/article/5g-health-risks-the-war-between-technology-and-human-beings?gclid=Cj0KCQjwsrWZBhC4ARIsAGGUJurFdcwDf4raFxBps6Hjss25XziX2sjKE3PjZNIq62x1_3hOnYWQb9MaAnQtEALw_wcB.

Schwab, Klaus. 2016. "The Fourth Industrial Revolution, by Klaus Schwab." World Economic Forum. 2016.
https://www.weforum.org/about/the-fourth-industrial-revolution-by-klaus-schwab.

Gates, Bill. n.d. "The Future of Progress." www.gatesfoundation.org. Accessed October 7, 2022.
https://www.gatesfoundation.org/goalkeepers/report/2022-report/#BillEssay.

Cohen, Ariel. 2021. "A Bill Gates Venture Aims to Spray Dust into the Atmosphere to Block the Sun. What Could Go Wrong?" Forbes. Accessed October 7, 2022.
https://www.forbes.com/sites/arielcohen/2021/01/11/bill-gates-backed-climate-solution-gains-traction-but-concerns-linger/?sh=30a09b1b793b.

Yarlagadda, Tara. 2021. "1 Big pro and 4 Cons of Solar Geo-engineering." Inverse.
https://www.inverse.com/science/solar-geoengineering-pros-and-cons.

"Even as Birth Rates Decline Overpopulation Remains a Global Challenge." 2018. World Economic Forum.
https://www.weforum.org/agenda/2018/04/almost-everywhere-people-are-having-fewer-children-so-do-we-still-need-to-worry-about-overpopulation/.

"This Is How Much People around the World Think Climate Change Is Impacting Their Lives." 2022. World Economic Forum.
https://www.weforum.org/agenda/2022/09/climate-change-severe-impacts-lives/.

Hannam, Paddy. 2021. "Stop Blaming Everything on Climate Change." www.spiked-Online.com. Accessed October 7, 2022.
https://www.spiked-online.com/2021/11/01/stop-blaming-every thing-on-climate-change/.

Nash, Ethan. 2020 "The Gates Family, Eugenics and COVID-19." VK. Accessed October 7, 2022.
https://vk.com/@secretxgovernment-the-gates-family-eugenics-and-covid-19.

"Eugenics Definition - Google Search." n.d. www.google.com.
https://www.google.com/search?client=safari&rls=en&q=eugenics+definition&ie=UTF-8&oe=UTF-8.

Gordon, L. 1974. "The Politics of Population: Birth Control and the Eugenics Movement." Radical America 8 (4): 61–98.
https://pubmed.ncbi.nlm.nih.gov/11615086/.

Joyce, Kathryn. 2020. "The Long, Strange History of Bill Gates Population Control Conspiracy Theories." Type Investigations.
https://www.typeinvestigations.org/investigation/2020/05/12/the-long-strange-history-of-bill-gates-population-control-conspir-acy-theories/.

Ahmed, Sharmeen. 2017. "Countries and the Effectiveness of Current Measures." Annual Survey of International & Comparative Law 22.

https://digitalcommons.law.ggu.edu/cgi/viewcontent.cgi?
article=1205&context=annlsurvey.

Chapter 22 – Is An Awakened World Possible?

"COVID-19'S Legacy: This Is How to Get the Great Reset Right." n.d.
World Economic Forum.
https://www.weforum.org/agenda/2020/07/covid19-this-is-how-
to-get-the-great-reset-right/.

Schwab, Klaus. 2016. "The Fourth Industrial Revolution, by Klaus
Schwab." World Economic Forum.
2016. https://www.weforum.org/about/the-fourth-industrial-
revolution-by-klaus-schwab.

Chapter 23 – Awakening Has Already Begun

Sinha-Hikim, Indrani, Stephen M Roth, Martin I Lee, and Shalender
Bhasin. 2003. "Testosterone-Induced Muscle Hypertrophy Is As
sociated with an Increase in Satellite Cell Number in Healthy,
Young Men." American Journal of Physiology. Endocrinology and
Metabolism 285 (1): E197-205.
https://doi.org/10.1152/ajpendo.00370.2002.

Rogers, Zachary. 2022. The National. 2022. "Calvin Klein Slammed
for 'Pregnant Man' in Mother's Day Commercial." WNWO.
May 13, 2022.
https://nbc24.com/news/nation-world/pregnant-trans-man-fea
tured-in-calvin-klein-mothers-day-commercial-draws-backlash-
roberto-bete-transgender-instagram-motherhood-outkick-alejan-
dro-avila-steven-crowder-intolerance.

Sunnucks, Mike. n.d. "CDC: COVID Vaccines Won't Stop Transmission; Fully Vaccinated Can Still Get, Spread Delta Strain." The Star
Democrat.
https://www.stardem.com/news/national/cdc-covid-vaccines-
won-t-stop-transmission-fully-vaccinated-can-still-get-spread-delta-
strain/article_5f83d0cb-8b0a-535d-bbad-3f571754e5ae.html.

BBC News. 2021. "Japan Finds Black Particles in Moderna Vaccine,"
September 1, 2021, sec. Asia.
https://www.bbc.com/news/world-asia-58405210.

Seneff, Stephanie, and Greg Nigh. 2021. "Worse than the Disease? Reviewing Some Possible Unintended Consequences of the MRNA Vaccines against COVID-19." https://dpbh.nv.gov/uploadedFiles/dpbhnvgov/content/Boards/BOH/Meetings/2021/SENEFF~1.PDF.

Bartlett, Tom. 2021. "The Vaccine Scientist Spreading Vaccine Misinformation." The Atlantic. August 12, 2021. https://www.theatlantic.com/science/archive/2021/08/robert-malone-vaccine-inventor-vaccine-skeptic/619734/. "Operation Warp Speed." 2021. Wikipedia. January 7, 2021. https://en.wikipedia.org/wiki/Operation_Warp_Speed.

"Doctors File First Lawsuit Challenging California Law That Seeks to Punish Physicians for COVID 'Misinformation.'" 2022. Children's Health Defense. Accessed October 7, 2022. https://childrenshealthdefense.org/defender/federal-lawsuit-california-punish-physicians-covid-misinformation/?itm_term=home.

Chapter 24 – Protect Our Children

Sood, Neeraj, and Jay Bhattacharya. 2021. "Mandatory Masking of School Children Is a Bad Idea." USC Schaeffer. July 16, 2021. https://healthpolicy.usc.edu/article/mandatory-masking-of-school-children-is-a-bad-idea/.

Spiegelman, Ian. 2021. "LA and San Diego School Districts Sue over Vaccine Mandates." Los Angeles Magazine. October 15, 2021. https://www.lamag.com/citythinkblog/l-a-and-san-diego-school-districts-are-being-sued-for-their-vaccine-mandates/.

"AG Paxton Sues Biden Administration for Silencing Parents, Labeling Them 'Terrorists.'" 2022. Texas Attorney General. Accessed October 10, 2022. https://www.texasattorneygeneral.gov/news/releases/ag-paxton-sues-biden-administration-silencing-parents-labeling-them-terrorists.

"Health Nightmare': Dr. Robert Malone Spotlights Study on MRNA Spike Protein." n.d. ClarkCountyToday.com. https://www.clarkcountytoday.com/news/health-nightmare-dr-robert-malone-spotlights-study-on-mrna-spike-protein/.

Senator. 2022. "Senator Wiener's Statement on Decision to Pull SB
866, Teens Choose Vaccines Act." Senator Scott Wiener.
August 31, 2022.
https://sd11.senate.ca.gov/news/20220831-senator-wiener%
E2%80%99s-statement-decision-pull-sb-866-teens-choose-
vaccines-act.

Chapter 25 – Conscious Evolution

Mary Parker Follet. 1998. The New State : Group Organization
the Solution of Popular Government.
Philadelphia: Pennsylvania State University Press.

Nelson, Gary M. 2016. "Mary Parker Follett – Creativity and
Democracy." Human Service Organizations: Management, Leadership & Governance 41 (2): 178–85.
https://doi.org/10.1080/23303131.2016.1263073.

Peek, Sean. 2018. "The Management Theory of Mary Parker Follett."
Business.com. 2018.
https://www.business.com/articles/management-theory-
of-mary-parker-follett/.

Myers, Steven Lee. 2022. "California Approves Bill to Punish Doctors
Who Spread False Information." The New York Times, August 30,
2022, sec. Technology.
https://www.nytimes.com/2022/08/29/technology/california-
doctors-covid-misinformation.html.

Pie, Bruce. 2021. "People of Future Will Have Microchips Implanted
in Their 'Brains' Says World Economic Forum Boss - the BL."
Accessed October 11, 2022.
https://thebl.com/us-news/people-of-future-will-have-microchips-
implanted-in-their-brains-says-world-economic-forum-boss.html.

Wagner, Kurt. 2016. "Mark Zuckerberg Has Finished Building His
Robot Butler, Jarvis." Vox. December 19, 2016.
https://www.vox.com/2016/12/19/14008196/mark-zuckerberg-
jarvis-butler-robot-house-facebook.

Shead, Sam. 2020. "Elon Musk Says DeepMind Is His 'Top Concern' When It Comes to A.I." CNBC. July 29, 2020. https://www.cnbc.com/2020/07/29/elon-musk-deepmind-ai.html.

Chapter 26 - The Future Is Here

Purdy, Chase. 2017. "Bill Gates Headlines an All-Star List of Investors Pumping $75 Million into Meatless Burgers." Quartz. August 2, 2017. https://qz.com/1044498/bill-gates-impossible-foods-investment-increases-in-meatless-burger-funding-round/.

Dr Joseph Mercola. 2021. "Vandana Shiva: Bill Gates Empires 'Must Be Dismantled' - Regeneration International." Regeneration International. April 5, 2021. https://regenerationinternational.org/2021/04/05/vandana-shiva-bill-gates-empires-must-be-dismantled/.

"Reject Bill Gates' Impossible Burger." 2022. **Organicconsumers.org. 2022.** https://www.organicconsumers.org/newsletter/biodemocracy-or-biofascism/reject-bill-gates%E2%80%99-impossible-burger.

Niassy, Saliou, and Sunday Ekesi. 2017. "Eating Insects Has Long Made Sense in Africa. The World Must Catch Up." The Conversation. January 11, 2017. https://theconversation.com/eating-insects-has-long-made-sense-in-africa-the-world-must-catch-up-70419.

Marcelo, Philip. 2022. "Bill Gates Owns a Lot of American Farmland, but Not the Majority." 2022. AP NEWS. May 2, 2022. https://apnews.com/article/fact-check-bill-gates-blac rock-788010130032.

Chapter 27 – How To Keep Consciousness Alive

Fatemi, Sayyed Mohsen and Kirk J. Schneider. 2019. "Today's Biggest Threat: The Polarized Mind." Scientific American Blog Network. https://blogs.scientificamerican.com/observations/todays-biggest-threat-the-polarized-mind/.

Stroebel, Duey. 2021. "Declaring War against Unvaccinated." https://legis.wisconsin.gov/senate/20/stroebel/media/

1678/091021-bidenabandonsconstitutionindeclaringwaragain-stunvaccinated.pdf

Chapter 28 – The Day The Earth Woke Up

Shermer, Michael. 2008. "Reel Life: The Day the Earth Stood Still."
Scientific American. Accessed October 12, 2022.
https://www.scientificamerican.com/article/review-day-the-earth-stood-still/.

Network, Earth Day. 2020. "The 50th Anniversary of Earth Day
Unites Tens of Millions of People across the World in Action and a
Multi-Platform Event."
www.prnewswire.com. Accessed October 12, 2022. https://www.
prnewswire.com/news-releases/the-50th-anniversary-of-earth-day-
unites-tens-of-millions-of-people-across-the-world-in-action-and-
a-multi-platform-event-301046887.html.

"Netherlands: The Summer of Discontent." 2022. The Spectator
Australia. July 28, 2022.
https://www.spectator.com.au/2022/07/netherlands-the-
summer-of-discontent/.

"Robert W Malone MD." n.d. Robert W Malone MD.
https://www.rwmalonemd.com/.

Loh, Matthew.2022. "Canada Says It Will Freeze the Bank Accounts
of 'Freedom Convoy' Truckers Who Continue Their Anti-Vaccine
Mandate Blockades." Business Insider.
https://www.businessinsider.com/trudeau-canada-freeze-bank-
accounts-freedom-convoy-truckers-2022-2.

Carroll, Patrick. 2022. "Amish Farmer Faces Fines, Prison Time for
Refusing to Comply with USDA Regulations | Patrick Carroll."
Fee.org. August 23, 2022.
https://fee.org/articles/amish-farmer-faces-fines-prison-time-for-
refusing-to-comply-with-usda-regulations/.

"United Nations Development Programme (UNDP)." n.d. Namati.
Accessed October 12, 2022.
https://namati.org/network/organization/united-nations-develop
ment-programme-undp/.

"SuperSummary." n.d. SuperSummary. Accessed October 12, 2022.
https://www.supersummary.com/an-inconvenient-truth/
summary/?utm_source=google&utm_medium=cpc&utm_
campaign=17311150304&utm_content=&utm_term=&gclid=
Cj0KCQjwhY-aBhCUARIsALNIC05qxbiLFYObTOMAybX-
7svc_-Ni7dVG58sRMdFwKwFPjgfPduxVDySsaAvr7EALw_wcB.

Chapter 29 – Who Will Lead the Way?

Ellerbeck, Stefan. 2022. "How Much Progress Is Being Made on
the UN's Sustainable Development Goals?" n.d. World Economic
Forum.
https://www.weforum.org/agenda/2022/09/un-sustainable-
development-goals-progress-report/.

Auken, Ida. 2016. "Welcome to 2030: I Own Nothing, Have No
Privacy and Life Has Never Been Better." Forbes.
Accessed October 12, 2022.
https://www.forbes.com/sites/worldeconomicforum/2016/11/10/
shopping-i-cant-really-remember-what-that-is-or-how-differently-
well-live-in-2030/?sh=7173fc9c1735.

"Abba Kovner." n.d. Encyclopedia.ushmm.org.
https://encyclopedia.ushmm.org/content/en/article/abba-kovner.

Chapter 30 – Realistic Utopianism

"Utopia - New World Encyclopedia." n.d.
www.newworldencyclopedia.org.
https://www.newworldencyclopedia.org/entry/utopia.

The Economic Times. 2022. "How the Metaverse Future May Look
like in 2030."
https://economictimes.indiatimes.com/markets/cryptocurrency/
how-the-metaverse-future-may-look-like-in-2030/article-
show/91175337.cms.

Auken, Ida. 2016. "Welcome to 2030: I Own Nothing, Have No
Privacy and Life Has Never Been Better." Forbes.
Accessed October 12, 2022.
https://www.forbes.com/sites/worldeconomicforum/2016/11/10/
shopping-i-cant-really-remember-what-that-is-or-how-differently-

well-live-in-2030/?sh=7173fc9c1735.

United Nations. 2015. "Sustainable Development Goals." United
Nations Sustainable Development. United Nations. 2015.
https://www.un.org/sustainabledevelopment/sustainable-
development-goals/.

Chapter 31 – Awaken To The Shadow

"Anthony Fauci Describes the 'Fauci Effect,' Brags He 'Symbolize[S]'
'Truth' on COVID." 2022.
www.youtube.com. Accessed October 12, 2022.
https://www.youtube.com/watch?v=bsJHKFmLsto.

Wedge, Marilyn. 2015. "The Surprising Shadow Side of a Narcissist.
Psychology Today."
www.psychologytoday.com. Accessed October 12, 2022.
https://www.psychologytoday.com/us/blog/suffer-the-chil-
dren/201507/the-surprising-shadow-side-narcissist.

Chapter 32 – Resisting The Singularity

Kurzweil, Ray. 2005. The Singularity Is near : When Humans
Transcend Biology. London: Duckworth.

Matthews, Dylan. 2019. "AI Disaster Won't Look like the Terminator.
It'll Be Creepier." Vox. March 26, 2019.
https://www.vox.com/future-perfect/2019/3/26/18281297/ai-
artificial-intelligence-safety-disaster-scenarios.

Chapter 33 – The Omega Point

"Omega Point." 2022. Wikipedia. August 31, 2022.
https://en.wikipedia.org/wiki/Omega_Point.

Castillo, M. 2011. "The Omega Point and Beyond: The Singularity
Event." American Journal of Neuroradiology 33 (3): 393–95.
https://doi.org/10.3174/ajnr.a2664.

Singh, Simran. 2022. "Analysing Thomas Eliot's (T.S. Eliot) Poems:
'the Hollow Men' and 'Preludes.'"

Owlcation. Accessed October 12, 2022.
https://owlcation.com/humanities/How-TS-Eliots-Poetry-

Explores-the-Relationship-Between-Individals-and-Their-World-
Part-Two.

Savage, Maddy. 2019. "NPR Choice Page." Npr.org. 2019.
https://www.npr.org/2018/10/22/658808705/thousands-of-
swedes-are-inserting-microchips-under-their-skin.

"Klaus Schwab. 2016. Implant Microchip, French with Engl.
Translation." n.d. www.youtube.com. Accessed October 12, 2022.
https://www.youtube.com/watch?v=GmmPVipAAio.

"The World Economic Forum Wants Children Microchipped!" n.d.
www.youtube.com. Accessed October 12, 2022.
https://www.youtube.com/watch?v=OgFaBGxppvs.

Ramirez, Vanessa Bates. 2022. "Flippy the Fast Food Robot Just
Got Hired in 100 Restaurants." Singularity Hub. February 17, 2022.
https://singularityhub.com/2022/02/17/flippy-the-fast-food-robot-
is-going-to-work-in-100-restaurants/.

"One-a-Day Comments on AI Quotes in Forbes: **Von Neumann.**" n.d.
Rage inside the Machine. Accessed October 12, 2022.
https://www.rageinsidethemachine.com/robert-elliott-smith/one-
a-day-comments-on-ai-quotes-in-forbes-von-neumann.

Chapter 34 – EQ Consciousness

"The EQ Test." n.d. **www.thepersonalitylab.org.**
Accessed October 12, 2022.
https://www.thepersonalitylab.org/eq-test?gclid=CjwKCAjwq-
JSaBhBUEiwAg5W9p8rXE2n522Qj8zAo8gBsk8A2GxUJyDPudW-
1cfg_-fPo0byX6JGFgehoCxRIQAvD_BwE.

Browne, Ed. 2021. "Fauci 'Untruthful' to Congress about Wuhan Lab
Research, Documents Suggest." 2021. Newsweek.
September 9, 2021.
https://www.newsweek.com/fauci-untruthful-congress-wuhan-
lab-research-documents-show-gain-function-1627351.

Crane, Emily. 2022. "Dr. Anthony Fauci Stepping down as NIAID
Chief, WH Medical Adviser in December." New York Post.
August 22, 2022.

https://nypost.com/2022/08/22/dr-anthony-fauci-to-step-down-from-his-post-in-december/.

Rees, Laurence. 2012. "Viewpoint: His Dark Charisma." BBC News, November 12, 2012.
https://www.bbc.com/news/magazine-20237437.

Chapter 35 – It Is Up To Us

"10 Times the Earth Was Almost Destroyed." n.d. www.history.com. Accessed October 12, 2022.
https://www.history.com/topics/ancient-history/earth-almost-destroyed-video.

"15 Times the World Was Almost Completely Destroyed - Opera News." n.d. opera.news. Accessed October 12, 2022.
https://ng.opera.news/ng/en/science/adcd34a002010ebf2878baebdd44106d.

Washington Post. 2022. "Opinion | Putin Threatens Nuclear War. The West Must Deter Disaster."
https://www.washingtonpost.com/opinions/2022/10/03/putin-nuclear-war-ukraine-deter/.

Newburger, Emma. 2022. "California Finds PG&E Equipment Responsible for Massive Dixie Fire." CNBC. January 5, 2022.
https://www.cnbc.com/2022/01/05/california-finds-pge-equipment-responsible-for-massive-dixie-fire-.html.

Lerner, Sharon, Mara Hvistendahl, Maia Hibbett. September 10 2021, and 1:03 A.m. "NIH Documents Provide New Evidence U.S. Funded Gain-of-Function Research in Wuhan." The Intercept.
https://theintercept.com/2021/09/09/covid-origins-gain-of-function-research/.

"Remdesivir, given to Half of Hospitalized Covid Patients in U.S., Is Big Win for Gilead — Boosted by Taxpayers." 2021. News-Medical.net. January 27, 2021.
https://www.news-medical.net/news/20210127/Remdesivir-given-to-half-of-hospitalized-covid-patients-in-US-is-big-win-for-Gilead-e28094-boosted-by-taxpayers.aspx.

Cohen, Jon and Kai Kupferschmidt 2020. "The 'Very, Very Bad Look' of Remdesivir, the First FDA-Approved COVID-19 Drug." www.science.org. https://www.science.org/content/article/very-very-bad-look-remdesivir-first-fda-approved-covid-19-drug.

Allen, Anna. 2022. "Pandemic Paid Off: Dr. Fauci's Net Worth Doubled during COVID." 2022. Washington Free Beacon. September 30, 2022. https://freebeacon.com/coronavirus/pandemic-paid-off-dr-faucis-net-worth-doubled-during-covid/.

Chapter 36 - Our New World

"Order Definition & Meaning I Britannica Dictionary." n.d. www.britannica.com. Accessed October 12, 2022. https://www.britannica.com/dictionary/order.

Hancock, Sam. 2021. "Australian Health Chief Uses Term 'New World Order' at Press Conference." The Independent. September 9, 2021. https://www.independent.co.uk/news/world/australasia/australia-new-world-order-conspiracies-b1917082.html.

Rolland, Nadège. 2020. "China's Vision for a New World Order: Implications for the United States." The National Bureau of Asian

Research (NBR). October 2, 2020. https://www.nbr.org/publication/chinas-vision-for-a-new-world-order-implications-for-the-united-states/.

Mauro, Aaron. 2020. "Coronavirus Contact Tracing Poses Serious Threats to Our Privacy." The Conversation. https://theconversation.com/coronavirus-contact-tracing-poses-serious-threats-to-our-privacy-137073.

Wells, H G. 1986. The War of the Worlds. Oxford ; Singapore ; Tokyo: Oxford University Press.

Holman, Stephen. 2019. "Meet the Associate Editors: Stephen Holman." Rapid Communications in Mass Spectrometry 33 (S3): 11–13. https://doi.org/10.1002/rcm.8364.

TIME TO AWAKEN

CHANGING THE WORLD WITH CONSCIOUS AWARENESS

ORA NADRICH

About The Author

Ora Nadrich is a pioneering Mindfulness expert, international keynote speaker, coach, and the founder and president of the Institute for Transformational Thinking. New York Times bestselling author, Marianne Williamson, has said, "When she speaks, I listen; when she writes, I read it; when she gives advice, I heed it." Ora is a sought-after expert in the fields of Mindfulness, transformational thinking, and self-discovery. Ora created and popularized her highly-effective "Says Who? Method", which allows her clients to ask simple questions that result in profound, personal and professional transformation.

Ora is the author of *"Says Who? How One Simple Question Can Change the Way You Think Forever"*, and *"Live True: A Mindfulness Guide to Authenticity"*, named one of the 100 Best Mindfulness Books of All Time" by BookAuthority, which is "the world's leading site for book recommendations by thought leaders", and recently was chosen as one of the top 5 books on authenticity in Positive Psychology. Her work has also been featured in Thrive Global, Fast Company, NBC News, Women's Health Magazine, Reader's Digest, Psychology Today, Yahoo! Health, Success Magazine, and many others. She is a frequent Huffington Post contributor and one of their leading global Mindfulness experts.

Ora and her book, *Mindfulness and Mysticism*, with a foreword by his Holiness the 14th Dalai Lama, were featured on KTLA News.